MASTER
MEDIA
LIMITED

MasterMedia books are available at a discount with bulk purchase for educational, group, premium, or sales promotion use. For information, please write or call:

Special Sales Department
MasterMedia Limited
333 West 52nd Street
Suite 306
New York, NY 10019
(212) 246-9500

MANAGING IT ALL

Time-Saving Ideas for Career, Family, Relationships & Self

BEVERLY BENZ TREUILLE
and
SUSAN SCHIFFER STAUTBERG

M A S T E R
M E D I A
L I M I T E D
New York

Published by MasterMedia Limited

MASTERMEDIA and colophon are registered trademarks of
MasterMedia Limited

10 9 8 7 6 5 4 3 2 1

Library of Congress Cataloging-in-Publication Data
Treuille, Beverly Benz.
Managing it all: time-saving ideas for career, family, relationships
and self / by Beverly Benz Treuille and Susan Schiffer Stautberg.
p.   cm.
ISBN 0-942361-09-1 (pbk.)
1. Women—United States—Time management.   2. Working
mothers—United States—Time management.   3. Working class
women—United States—Time management.   4. Women executives—
United States—Time management.   5. Time management
surveys.   I. Stautberg, Susan Schiffer.
HQ1221.T755   1988
640'.43'088042—dc19   88-8364
CIP

Designed by Irving Perkins Associates

Manufactured in the United States of America

To our families:
Antoine, Adrien, Geneviève, and Philippe
B.B.T.

Edward and Ted
S.S.S.

ACKNOWLEDGMENTS

We would like to thank the following people who were among the many who contributed to this book.

Kathy Adams
Randy Allen
Carol Lewis Anderson
Eugenia Anderson-Ellis
Kristina Andersson
Nancy Aranow
Elaine Arnold
Marguerite Dixon Ayers
Carole Barriquand
Susan Beer
Eve Benton
Jewel Huber Benz
Joyce Black
Polly Boe
Carole Boulanger
Judith Briles
Clare P. Buden
Rita Burgelman
Marie-Claude Butler
Dianne Butt
Margaret Cannella
Marcia Cantarella
Sandra Cassel
Sally Dayton Clement
Aletha Cuscaden
Joan Dacey-Seib
Tian Dayton

Françoise Desbrez
Brigitte Dunoyer
Barbara Evans
Annelie Fahlstedt
Andree Favereau
Claire Fountain
Arlyn Gardner
Fabianne Gershon
Phyllis Gillis
Susan Gilmore
Kathryn Goldfrank
Beth Greenfeld
Eva Griegg
Rosalinda Guerra
Nancy Hathaway
Sue Hipkins
Mary Onie Holland
Karen Elliott House
Julia Jitkoff
Janet Jones-Parker
Belinda Kaye
Virginia Keim
Benedicte Kosciusko-Morizet
Cele G. Lalli
Jennetta Lambert
Andrea H. Lambrinides
Joan Layton

Mariana S. Leighton
Ellen Levine
Florence Liddell
Dr. Jeanette Lofas
Pamela Loree
Blanche Mansfield
Cindy Mascone
Magdaleine Mathiot
Rebecca Matthias
Wendy L. McAfoose
Joan McMenamin
Dr. Pam Neuman
Joyce Newman
Melanie Niemiec
Barbara Nolan
Jane O'Connor
Mary Ousley
Virginia Perrette
Lucille Peyrelongue
Emily Rafferty
Eleanor Raynolds, C.B.E.
Rose Lee Reinhard

Jean-Marie Renard
Sally Richards
Kathy Robinson
Annie-Claude Roche
Annette Rodriguez
Steven R. Schubert
Rae Paige Schwarz
Jacqueline Simon
Robin Smith
Nadia Spencer
Linda Stern
Robin Straus
Mavis Taintor
Florence Tatistcheff
Linda Taylor
Christine Thomas
Colette Treuille
Bette Warshawsky
Hester Weeden
Anne Wilkinson
Kristi Witker

CONTENTS

AUTHORS' PREFACE

Although we are the authors of this book, *Managing It All* is actually the work of hundreds of women who are both parenting and pursuing careers. We sent questionnaires to women throughout the United States, as well as in foreign countries, and asked them how *they* manage it all. What advice do they have for other women facing the same dilemma—the same busy lives, the same lack of time, the same stresses. The response was overwhelming. Women were anxious to share their experiences, successes, and failures in order to help others who are struggling to create the best possible lives—both personally and professionally—for their families and themselves.

Our book addresses mothers (and fathers) as a group, but you should evaluate the ideas and hints based on your own unique family situation. A mother of three children may smile when a mother of only one child laments the rarity of the moments they have together. A person in a happy marriage only dimly perceives what it means to raise children alone. Parents of adolescents often have forgotten what it means to care for a toddler.

Our respondents represent every category of family situation: intact families with from one to six children, single parent families, large families resulting from the remarriage of each spouse and subsequent additions, parents of newborns and grown children, parents of children with learning disabilities, medical problems, or unique talents.

The multitude of career and job environments presents another spectrum of pressure and rewards: time demands and the necessity for flexibility, training requirements, the need to keep one's foot in the door. We received replies from women who know all about the problems of work and family, women who are engaged in all sorts of careers: opera singers and lawyers, literary agents and research scientists. They know about trying to make progress in a work environment, while still finding time to be there for their husbands and children.

Some of our respondents are fast-trackers, going all out for success. Others are women with less-demanding jobs, who are trying to help support their families financially and emotionally. The pressures are there for all women, and the need to find better ways to achieve their goals unites them.

We used in-depth interviews, formal and informal, to deepen our understanding of how the busy woman manages to keep her job and her equilibrium. We interviewed not only the women themselves, but also those near to them, those able to observe the effects of managing it all: husbands, parents, grandparents, children, bosses, employees, school administrators. Teenagers and school principals were especially helpful in providing perspective on what it means to be—or to have—a working mother.

There are numerous books and articles about the problems of the working parent: Should a parent work? Will the family suffer? Can you expect to reach the summit in your field if you have priorities other than your career? This book *starts* with the assumption that you have—or want to have—a job and family . . . and that you want to manage better.

The value of this book lies in its immediacy and practicality. Our material can take the place of the traditional village well—where the women gather to exchange ideas and discuss problems and their solutions with others in the same situation. If *Managing It All* can provide you with just a few new ideas on how *you* can manage better in your life, we feel that we have been successful.

We hope that this book will be a great help to you in finding more time, quality time. Even as we go to press, wonderful ideas are pouring in from all over. Won't you share your thoughts and ideas with us, too? Your suggestions may be the sanity-savers or delightful discoveries for others who are doing what you are doing—managing it all.

MANAGING
IT ALL

INTRODUCTION

Time is "the most valuable thing a man can spend," and, though infinite, "once lost, it is never found again." So counseled sages through the centuries—the Greek Diogenes Laertius, and the American Benjamin Franklin. From the beginning of recorded history, we have pondered the nature of time and tried to understand it.

In today's frenetic world, thoughts about time—lost and found—have both profound and practical meaning.

According to market research, the complaint among Americans about lack of time is widespread. Most adults feel that they don't have enough time to do everything they want to do; many state they'd like to have more time with family or friends. Time pressure is the reason most cited for stress between husbands and wives.

We each get twenty-four hours a day—no more, no less—regardless of age, sex, income, or intelligence. It is how we *manage* our time that is critical, not only to what we accomplish but to the quality of our lives.

Probably no group in contemporary society experiences the stress of "not enough time" more than the modern American woman who is attempting to combine career and family, while still retaining a little time for herself. Working women end up with about ten hours less free time per week than either housewives or employed men. While women who are not employed spend an average of forty hours a week on housework, employed women spend only twenty-six—but those twenty-six hours are in addition to an outside work commitment of at least forty hours a week!

Women with families, trying to manage households while carpooling and shopping and volunteering in their communities, want more time. Career women juggling full-time jobs, business trips, and husbands waiting at home want more time. Women who are single parents want more time. The fact is, we all want more time!

Despite the difficulties in managing it all, most women would not give up the new options and opportunities won by the women's movement in exchange for less interesting lives and few demands on their time. If we are going to manage it all, the responsibility is largely ours (with help from the men in our lives) to make our choices work. Managing time is really learning to manage ourselves.

"Managing it all" doesn't mean *doing* it all or *having* it all. It doesn't mean becoming a victim of the "superwoman" myth. It means making choices about what is important to you, setting goals, establishing priorities—and sticking to them. It also means learning flexibility and the ability, sometimes, to do nothing, to think, to daydream. It means getting to know and appreciate yourself—the strengths you can build on and the weaknesses you can strive to overcome. It means working smarter, not harder. It means learning to say no nicely. It means learning to manage your time rather than letting it manage you. Ironically, when you eliminate the stress of trying to do *everything*, when you concentrate on what you can accomplish, you'll do more of what you really need and want to do in life!

Time management is not a goal in itself. Its purpose is to enable us to get the most out of the time we spend—not only the most productivity, but also the most satisfaction. People who achieve professional goals while sacrificing health and personal relationships are not effective time managers. Workaholics, with their narrow inward focus, are prime candidates for burnout. Effective time management should enable you not only to meet your professional goals, but to enrich your personal life as well. Ultimately, managing time means taking responsibility for the quality of our lives.

While there is no single right way to manage your time, time management can be learned. Often that means un-learning poor habits and substituting more systematized ways of doing things. It is part attitude, part technique, part practice. This book offers thousands of effective ways to do just that. It is the result of extensive research interviews with women, married and single, career women and job holders, who are mostly succeeding, occasionally struggling, to combine their careers and family life. They are women who have learned from experience and are making their own busy lives work. What they have learned to manage, you can too.

The purpose of this book is not to have you adopt every timesaving or quality-producing hint offered. It is to get you to think of time as a resource at your disposal—but one not to be wasted. Take the ideas that fit you and your situation, adapt them, work on those that don't come naturally but that you believe can be helpful. Remember there is often no right or wrong way to do things, simply better or worse ways—for you.

CHAPTER ONE

Time Management

There is no single system or rule that will guarantee to each woman the ability to juggle family, home, and career successfully. The techniques that work for one woman may be losing strategies for another. A solution that works well in one industry or one family may be totally wrong in another situation.

You will need to pick and choose among the ideas in this book, the advice of friends and relatives, and the wealth of suggestions in magazine and newspaper articles. The first steps are to be aware of your personal style and of the dynamics of your career field.

PERSONAL STYLE

"Know thyself" is a familiar but often ignored maxim. Have you taken the time to reflect on your personal style and on the implications for your career and family life? Take a survey of your personal situation and style.

7

e jugglers—love to have several balls in
They thrive on activity and seem to have
sually there is a strong inner sense of
ch may or may not be apparent to the
you are a juggler, here are some thoughts:

- ₁ₒᵤ   be well organized and to communicate your
  organization to others. Otherwise, you may drive your
  staff and family crazy, not to mention dropping balls at
  home and work. Use lists and calendars effectively to
  help those around you.
- Your style is well suited to a professional: lawyer, investment banker, entrepreneur, teacher. You can be involved
  in multiple projects and issues at work. At home, your
  ability to thrive under chaos can help tremendously,
  especially with young children.
- You *risk* undertaking too much and burning out. Watch
  for signs of stress in yourself, your family, and your co-
  workers. Make the necessary changes in your life before
  a crisis hits.

A second style is the *analyst*—one who undertakes each
task sequentially, preferring to finish each project before
undertaking the next. The analyst is effective and easy to
work with, at home and work. If you are the analyst:

- You will fit well into a large, multilayered organization.
  Your style meshes with others in a structured environment. At home, as at work, there is great clarity and
  purposefulness.
- You may be disturbed by interruptions and changes in
  plans. Select a job where you can pursue each task dili-
  gently. As you rise up the ladder and have greater control over your time, you will find increasing satisfaction
  in your work.

- Take advantage of your ability to get things done and your leadership qualities to manage projects—at home and work.

The *philosopher* never seems to be rushed or stressed. Each person or activity gets her full attention. Warm and sensitive, the philosopher gets along very well in family life and in creative careers. If you are a philosopher:

- Your lack of aggressive behavior may be viewed as low achievement. Avoid jobs such as sales, where activity is often equated with success. The philosopher can be extremely effective and creative without apparent stress.
- Your strength is dealing with people, so pick a career with high people content.
- You are *not* without stress, but are able to internalize or mask stress. Just be careful not to put too much pressure or responsibility on yourself.

While few of us are exclusively one type or another, we can all benefit by knowing our primary style. By capitalizing on the strong points of our style, and avoiding the pitfalls, we can best adapt our time management techniques to our lives.

You can also strive for balance in your personal style. If you feel that you are too strongly in one category, try to modify your behavior and draw on the best points of the other styles. The most successful woman may be the one who is the juggler when working alone, the analyst when working with others, and the philosopher when at home with the family.

In addition to style, your personal time clock and rhythm are important to consider when making both long- and short-range plans.

Morning people leap out of bed with no alarm, jog five

miles before breakfast, eat well, and arrive early for work, refreshed and ready to go. However, they have low points during the day, perhaps before lunch, in the late afternoon, and at 9:00 P.M. If you're a morning person:

- Schedule meetings and difficult projects for early in the morning or right after lunch. Save more relaxed items—going through your in-box or returning phone calls—for your low points.
- Don't try to accomplish too much over business meals or in the evening. They're not your prime times. Save these times to unwind and keep up with family and personal relationships.
- Jobs with excessive travel and entertaining are not for you.

Afternoon people do well during the normal working day, with peak performance in mid-morning and mid-afternoon. They fit well in the classic nine-to-five job. Their problem is that a significant change in pattern, such as an overnight flight or a sleepless night with a sick child, may throw their rhythm into a tailspin.

- Your high performance during the workday is a great asset. You don't have to schedule around periods of low energy, and can therefore plan a full workday and relaxed evening.
- Select a job with fairly regular hours and predictable travel. You may choose to work through lunch or have business lunches, saving personal activities for after work.
- Watch out for late-night work, crazy travel schedules, and business dinners that drag on and on. You have been at peak performance all day and can't expect to be able to continue the pace late into the evening. You need relaxed time to unwind and be with family and friends.

Night people resent getting up and are not fully functional until a requisite amount of caffeine has been ingested. They begin to really roll an hour before lunch and often can't be stopped until the wee hours of the morning. Suggestions for night people:

- Your ability to work unflaggingly in the evening can be a great asset in careers with important deadlines, such as consulting. In fields with a lot of travel, the time from lunch through the evening may be the keys to success. You can schedule flights to sleep on the plane, even in the morning.
- Your schedule may make it more difficult for you to work well in a nine-to-five environment. Working with morning people may be very difficult for you.
- When you start a family, you may be surprised to find yourself becoming more of a morning person, since that's the rhythm of a baby or small child. Anticipate this possible change in your time clock, and be sensitive to your own need for sleep and rest.

FAMILY STRUCTURE

Each family structure creates its own demands and rewards. Most of us will move through several different family structures through time. Take advantage of the opportunities afforded from each, and be aware of the pitfalls.

- The single woman with no children has the greatest opportunity to pursue a career at top speed and to leap up the corporate ladder several rungs at a time. If you want to be on the fast track, now is the time to maximize your ascent. Being single and childless also allows far greater risk-taking in both personal and career decisions. Move to a new city. Take a job with lots of travel. Begin a doctoral program. Take advantage of this time of maximum flexibility to really get your career off to a running start.

- Married or in a permanent relationship? You will now make decisions together and need to maximize the good for you as a couple. Make time for each other, and keep lines of communication open. The relative freedom of having no children, combined with security and stability in your personal life, makes this an ideal time for success in your career.

- As a young parent, be you twenty years old or forty, you are suddenly thrust into a triangle where one angle (the baby) has no desire or ability to compromise for the good of the group. Suddenly, you are at the mercy of naps and nappies. Thank goodness for maternity leave, which provides at least a few weeks to adjust to the new family structure with a child at its center.

- Most women find that they can keep up their careers at nearly the same pace as before they had the baby if they so choose. Child care for one child is generally affordable. You and your husband can take turns with the child to give each other some personal time. You can really enjoy your baby on mornings, evenings, weekends, and vacations, and can gear your adult schedule around the changing schedule of the baby.

- When you are expecting your first child, you should decide your plan for your career—full speed ahead, some slow-down, or stopping for the time being. But be prepared to adjust your plans after you've experienced the joys and pains of motherhood. Many avid career women find themselves unable to tear themselves away from their new babies. And many mothers who cher-

ished the idea of staying home find themselves restless
and bored without the challenges and stimulation of
their work.

- If your job entails a great deal of travel, late work, or
unpredictable hours, when you have a child you will
need to create a failproof safety net for child care and
nurturing. Hopefully, the father is willing to shoulder
much of the responsibility. If not, you may need to
rethink your career and child care options.

- The second child "makes it a family," according to some
parents. It also throws a monkey wrench into the idyllic
triangle that you heretofore enjoyed. While one child is
napping, the other is frolicking. There is little quiet time
in the home, and child care may be twice as expensive.
Still, there is one parent per child and each child can
enjoy a full measure of attention, even in a two-career
family.

- With two children, it is far harder to manage the fast
track than with one. Many women decide to accept more
gradual career progress in exchange for more time at
home; some turn to alternatives such as part-time work.
However, many very successful women have two children . . . or more!

"When I was pregnant with my first child, I decided to
take a long maternity leave (eight months) and then to
return to my career in finance, hopefully on the same
fast track I had left. During the leave, I got pregnant
again and had to rethink my plans. I went back to work
on time, but in a part-time position. I don't regret at all
slowing down to enjoy my children!"

- Should you decide to have three or more children, you
will probably find that managing a full-time fast-track

career is very difficult unless you have a staff at home to
handle everything for the children and household.
Alternatively, you may switch into a lower gear for the
time being. If you find that a very demanding or tiring
job, or a job with a long commute, puts too great a strain
on the family, be prepared to slow down or stop if necessary *before* everything falls apart.

CAREER DYNAMICS

Good time management requires you to take into account
certain dynamics of your career when you set goals and plan
for the future, as well as in day-to-day decisions about time
allocation and stress management.

The first parameter is control: to what extent are you able
to determine how to use your time, as opposed to having
others decide for you? In general, your control will go up as
you move up an organization. A clerk may have less control
than an administrative assistant, who in turn will be less in
control of her time than her boss. There are also fields where
you have more or less control of your time, regardless of
your level:

- High control is in fields where independent work is
  involved and deadlines or quotas are self-imposed.
- Medium control is often found in large organizations.
  Deadlines and targets may be dictated by the organization, but you have control over how you reach the goal.
- Low control is a problem in many assistant jobs. You may
  not have the authority to decide which tasks to undertake and when, so you do them all. There may be no one
  below you to delegate to. You may simply have to work

each day until all of the tasks piled on your desk are done.

- Low control is also felt in fields where the interests or needs of the client are paramount, and your own needs and interests are subordinate.

If you have a great deal of control, time management techniques can be invaluable to you. A savings of 10 percent of your time at work can result in the equivalent of *five "found" work weeks* per year!

A low level of control over time leaves you far fewer opportunities for applying time management techniques at work. In the short term, work on *stress*—the inevitable result of no time and no control—and apply good time management techniques at home. At the same time, take the long-term steps needed to get into a position where you have more control and can keep stress at an acceptable level.

Can you change the time requirements or stress in your job? In the short term, you may have little power to change the situation; in the long term, almost everyone can make adjustments or even radical changes in time and stress aspects of their jobs and lives.

- "He who has the gold makes the rules." If you are the boss, you already have the power. Implement changes that will improve the time and stress aspects of your job, *and* the jobs of your subordinates. If you are stressed to the point of poor performance, hire an assistant. If your staff is overworked: reallocate tasks, prioritize projects, work harder on developing cooperative team spirit.
- If you have little or no power—a rigid or unsympathetic boss, an unrealistic workload or excessive overtime—it is up to you to define your priorities and long-range plans and to get out of a situation that is not leading you in the right direction.

SETTING GOALS

The key to managing time efficiently is to have a clear idea of what you want to accomplish—your goals. You must figure out what you want to do with your professional and personal lives, and also the relative importance of each goal you set—your priorities.

The process of setting goals and priorities brings into focus what is important to you and what is not. It helps you make hundreds of choices about how you will use your time. You learn to accomplish the things that are most necessary to you, and not to fill your days with inconsequential tasks that lead nowhere.

Set time frames for your goals and periodically revise them. There are trade-offs—you can't have everything right away—but the choices are yours. Your desires and ambitions change over time. By adjusting goals to shifting life situations, you retain control by determining what is most important to you and going after it.

Setting goals is not an abstract task. There are certain practical steps that you can follow that will help you formulate your goals.

- Focus on the present. Your past offers a share of happy memories and a share of lessons learned. Your future promises some achievements and rewards, and probably some hard times. But it is the *present* that should be your primary focus—your life *now.* Think about what makes you happy—where your satisfactions lie. What do you want to eliminate from your life? Add? Change? Writing it down can be an important first step in setting your goals.

- Establish short-term, perhaps five-year, goals: the work you want to do, the house or apartment you want to live in, the courses you want to pass, the trip you want to take. Then ask yourself what you have to do to get there.
- Set goals that are measurable, that have a beginning and an end. You might want to lose ten pounds, accumulate family savings of $25,000 as a down payment on a house or condominium, learn French. If you know when you've reached a goal, it will make the achievement even more satisfying.
- Set *realistic* goals. If you have no chance of succeeding at one specific thing, cut it back to realistic size or leave it off your list. If you'll never be president of your firm, set your sights on vice president. You are too old to try for your ideal of four children? Then raise your two in the best way you know how. Probably won't be governor? Tend to your law practice—you never know what will happen.
- Set a tentative time limit for the completion of each goal. If you had planned to take courses in library science, and three years have gone by and you haven't even registered, it's time to rethink that goal. Be honest. Maybe you really don't want to be a librarian. Maybe you like your job in the bookstore so much that you'd like to open one of your own someday.
- Write down your goals and strategies for achieving them. The process is a kind of commitment and makes them more real and achievable.
- Don't be afraid to revise your list. Review your progress often—perhaps once a month. Have you at least started on each project on your list? Learned to use your personal computer? Chosen new curtains for the dining room? Updated your résumé? If months go by and you don't make a start toward a particular goal, ask yourself if your timing and strategy are realistic.

- If you have a family, goal-setting should be done to-gether. Your husband and older children will be impor-tant in setting both personal and family goals. Learn flexibility and how to compromise. Include the family in key decisions that will affect them. If you are going back to school, they ought to feel that they had some in-put into this decision. Their lives will be changed, too— there will certainly be less of you to go around.

You have a great job as an attorney in a fine law firm. Your husband is a physicist and needs a certain high-tech machine for his work that exists at only two univer-sities in the country. What do you do if he's offered a position at one of those institutions? Do you pack up the family and move? Do you suggest a long-distance marriage for a while till he's sure he likes the new position? . . .

You have been able to accept a challenging new pro-ject at work because your teenager has agreed to care for younger siblings for the summer. Suddenly, the teenager is given the opportunity to study film-making in China for July and August. Do you bow out of the project? Ask the teen to stay home? . . .

Your knee has been giving you problems. Several doctors agree that the sooner you have an operation, the better the chances that you will be able to walk without limping for the rest of your life. You will be "out of commission" for months—unable to work or care for the children. Do you wait till your financial resources make it easier and your preschooler is in school, or do you do it now? . . .

THIS IS THE TIME FOR A FAMILY MEETING!

A couple in Boston with two boys, ten and twelve, found their dream house—a turn-of-the-century Victorian that needed a lot of work. After a home improvement loan, they were ready to produce a masterpiece. But after only four months, when they realized that their scheme of heating the house with a coal stove was not going to work, and the stove pipe covering in the basement turned out to be asbestos and had to be removed by experts at great expense, and the job they did stripping the stairs down to the original oak looked just awful, and the boys were no help at all, they decided to reprioritize. Their goal to have the perfect house some day fell to the bottom of their list, until they could afford some hired labor. They sold the house to a well-off older couple who were going to use it on weekends and not do any of the renovation themselves. They bought a newish development house in a Boston suburb. It was clean and neat and came with a microwave oven and a sauna. They don't see this move as forever, but for a few years at this stage in their lives it seems ideal.

- If you've had any serious resistance from family members, ease into your new project. Enroll in one course until your spouse and children become accustomed to the idea of Mom hitting the books after dinner while they wash the dishes. Too much change *may* shake the equilibrium of your family and cause so much upset that you'll never get anything done.
- If your goal entails a major long-term change—renovating your old house yourself on weekends, which involves a lot of sweat equity and will take about two years—try

to imagine specifically what it will mean to your family.
Have you thought about stepping in paint cans and
sawdust, and having unattached sinks in the middle of
the living room because the plumber didn't show up?
Month after month? If you can't stand chaos and your
kids are too small to wield a hammer, you might want to
rethink this goal, at least for the moment.

PLANNING

Once goals have been thought through, you are ready to
plan. The planning process can involve the participation of
your entire family. It should be reviewed, honed, improved
regularly. Some things to consider during the planning
stage:

- Is the plan in the best interest of all members of your
  family? Will it be especially hard on one member—
  perhaps too hard? Think of the high school senior who
  is suddenly uprooted to live in another state. You may
  have to compromise. If the family really must move,
  it might be better to make alternate living arrangements for your senior so he or she can finish out the
  year.
- Is a plan unusually risky? Are you perhaps staking all
  your money and your in-laws' money and the funds
  you've put away for your children's education on a fried-
  chicken franchise on the highway? What happens if it
  fails? When you plan your future, don't forget that a
  fall-back plan is necessary. If the risks seem too great,
  you might want to rethink your idea.
- Is your plan feasible? It's much wiser to divide any long-
  range goal into manageable steps. If you are obese, just

thinking of losing fifty pounds may cause you to panic and seek consolation with a chocolate donut. But five pounds doesn't seem impossible, or one pound a month. Can't make anything out of your new computer system with its bundled software? Learn one program at a time, and if you're still in trouble, take a weekend computer course. You *will* pick it up. Don't focus on the seven years of night courses till you get your M.B.A. Your plan is to have mastered corporate finance by next June.

We know of a book editor who always wanted to be a psychotherapist. While still employed, she took advantage of the educational benefits offered by her corporation and took courses in psychology—at night, one a semester. The semesters piled up, she earned her Ph.D., and could start her new career. An example of making excellent use of time in small increments!

- You must remain flexible. What if someone else in your town has the same thought of selling pickled watermelon rind to your few gourmet food shops? No room for *your* rind. Learn to pickle something else.

IMPLEMENTATION

When it comes to actually putting a plan into action, the implementation stage, trouble may arise. You should try to approach any difficulty with a positive problem-solving attitude. *You* set up the system; *you* can make it work.

- Have you thought through the details? Did you plan your new custom knitting business without giving enough thought to where you would get the knitters? Don't spend another penny until you have the people lined up.
- Do you procrastinate? The trick to getting a job started is to divide it into smaller bits, some of which you can delegate to family or hired workers. Once you get *something* accomplished and you see a project start to take shape, it should be easier to continue to completion.
- Some of your plans, of course, will not work out. You may have been too ambitious, or you may encounter unforeseen obstacles (for example, you may be overpowered by larger companies), or you may find your project hideously boring. Cut your losses, and forget about it.
- Is your family frantic from too *much* activity? Remember balance. You can have too many short- and long-term goals. Your plans can be too complex or your implementation too pressured. If none of you has a moment to sit and look at the flowers, then try to cut back—as a family and as individuals. You don't want to rush through life without knowing where you've been.

CHAPTER TWO

Getting Organized

There are, no doubt, people in the business world who function without the diaries, notepads, appointment books, stick-on slips, or miscellaneous scraps of paper that usually accompany us wherever we go. These *aides-mémoires* tell most of us where we're supposed to be, what we're supposed to be doing, and with whom. We need a lot of help in getting through an average day, and conventional wisdom says that if you don't want to forget it, *write it down.*

Here are some basic methods of organization. Remember, each system of organization must be personalized in order to *really* work for you. Some people arrange their time by writing lists on legal pads and index cards; others use the computer; still others use whatever is convenient, such as brown paper bags and Crayolas. If you don't have a well-organized system, start one.

- Don't look at your lists and diaries with fear—they are there to help you, not to overwhelm. They are there to work *for* you, even if they seem at times to have lives of their own.

- *Make* your lists and appointment books actually work. We all have days that get completely out of hand, in which nothing gets done, but if day follows day and your to-do lists remain untouched, something is wrong with your organization system. Rethink your list-making and scheduling techniques from top to bottom.
- Tailor-make your organization system. Suit *your* natural pace at home and the office. Allow for lifestyle needs that are uniquely yours. For example, does your spouse get home early from work two days a week? Then perhaps you can schedule a tennis game during that time, or a regular visit to an elderly parent.
- Organize and prioritize. Don't face each morning with a list the length of a Chinese scroll and an appointment scheduled every half hour. You won't be able to attend to 4,006 items. Organize your life into manageable segments.

LISTS

To clarify your thinking, a system of three different kinds of lists may be helpful.

- The first is a *master list*. The long-term goals that you set are here, in order of priority or time horizon. Do you want to have a house in the country within five years? Be head of your department when your boss retires in two years? Learn Spanish?
- Writing down your goals on a master list becomes a formal announcement of intent. It makes the goals real, and keeps them in the forefront of your mind. The goals are not cast in bronze. Be flexible. Review and revise your master list every three to six months.

- Keep duplicates of your master list. It could be at home, in your office desk drawer, on your computer. It keeps your plans in front of your eyes. And if you lose the one that you carry with you, you will at least have fairly recent thinking about your schedule.

A second list, the *projects list,* covers plans that you will have to deal with in the plannable future—during the next few weeks or months. This projects list is considerably more detailed, and helps start to implement your long-range goals.

- If you're unable to cope with a projects list that has instructions both to "assign cover art for the annual report" and to "make appointment for auto engine overhaul in February," then divide it into personal and business categories. List personal tasks on the left side of the paper, business projects on the right—and a thick, solid line in between. Alternatively, write business tasks on one side of a sheet or card and personal lists on the flip side. They will both be in the same general space, but effectively separated.

Don't be afraid to combine business and personal lists. You will find that when you're passing through an international airport on business and your connecting flight is six hours late, it is useful to have your Christmas shopping list on hand as you wander through the duty-free shops.

Your work section of this list must include:

- What the project is.
- If it has top priority.

- Are there related projects that also must be completed?
- When it is due.
- Your personal half of this list can be in shorthand: "Make dentist appt. for J. & T." or "Tax forms" or "Mom's b'day." (The names of your children do not have to be spelled out for you to recall them.)
- The organization of your projects list depends very much on the nature of your business. If you are in clothing design, you might want to organize your list seasonally; if you're in magazine publishing, monthly; a lawyer, case by case.

Use your projects list for three main purposes:

- To focus your master plan and to begin the early stages of your long-range goals.
- To help clarify your thinking. As you review the projects list, priorities and scheduling necessities become more obvious as you fit together the puzzle of the upcoming weeks.
- To function as the feeder for your daily to-do list, the basic tool that's with you in the front lines.

A daily *to-do list* is your third list—a micro-list that acts as a guide for the minutes and hours of the day that is beginning *now*.

- Make this a detailed list. Include all your chores and responsibilities for the day, both personal and professional. Many find it convenient to divide this list into three categories: people to call, people to see, or things to do.
- Know your priorities. Your most important tasks go at the top of the list. Start the day by reviewing your list and picking several items from it to dispose of right away.

- Remember your personal rhythm. Are you a morning person? Then the most important tasks should be done early, even if you have to get to the office before anyone else arrives to have some uninterrupted thinking time. If you *never* have uninterrupted thinking time at the office, then do the task at home from 5:30 to 8:30 A.M., and come in a little late.
- If your to-do list is as long after work as it was in the morning, go home and let your family know that they're on their own and you're off limits. There's no reason why they can't occasionally feed themselves and even bring you a snack on a tray!

You will save countless hours if you take the time to teach children rudimentary cooking. Children like it, and will be able to fend for themselves if you're detained at the office or have to spend your evening working at home.

An attorney who lives in Boston told us that in order for her to get through law school, when she was in her thirties and her children were eight, ten, and twelve, super-organizing was necessary. One night a week each child took on the responsibility of planning and cooking dinner for the family, although the eight-year-old had the help of Dad. Her lawyer husband did major weekly shopping and took his turn in the kitchen, too. She says, "At first I felt guilty when I saw eight-year-old Andrew standing on a stepstool to reach his wok—he usually cooked stir-fried vegetables and chicken—but we managed, and I can see now that my children are unusually self-reliant."

- The larger undertakings from your projects list should be broken down into manageable segments. Divide a major assignment that is on your projects list into day-by-day tasks for your to-do list. Set your deadline, and then work backward from that date. Plan to do a little each day in a logical sequence until the project is completed. Build in time for unavoidable delays.

- Draw a fine line between what ought to go on your daily list and what you can take for granted as being part of most days. "Read the paper" does not belong. Either you do read it every day because you really have to, or you find time for it when you can. Either way, you probably don't need a special reminder.
- Cross out or check off tasks as you complete them. This gives you a visible sense of progress and a record of the day's activities.
- Writing the project down on your daily to-do list is *not* the same as doing it. Sometimes just seeing "Do quarterly budget for support staff" on a neat, white paper gives the impression that you've actually gotten started. You haven't. Your goal is to cross it out!
- If a task remains undone day after day, rethink the schedule. If there is no immediate deadline, take it off the daily list and put it back on the projects list, until the time when you can fit it into your schedule realistically.
- The items on your lists should balance each other. Do not get so caught up in writing a major report that you do not return phone calls for days. No matter how high a priority a particular project has, the most important nuts and bolts of daily life still have to be tended.
- Try not to be stressed by changed plans. Build in some unplanned time as you write your daily list, or make sure that some of the projects can realistically be postponed a day or two. Learn from your past experiences. Expect outside forces to impinge—they always do. Be realistic about allocating enough time for each task. Just

Learn to use small amounts of time productively—
those five or ten minutes of unexpected freedom that
never appear on a daily list. You could:
• Call home to make sure all is well.
• Clean out a couple of files.
• Set up a business meeting.
• Make a doctor's appointment for you or a member of
your family.
• Plan the games for a child's birthday party.
• Write a short memo.
• Review the status of a project with a member of your
staff.
• Go through your in-box and reexamine your day's
priorities.
• Start to outline a speech.
• Do isometric exercises.
• Just stare into space and recharge your batteries.

because you want a meeting to take ten minutes, doesn't
mean it's going to. When it doesn't, you play catch-up
all day, feeling more and more stressed as the hours
fly by.
• Review your lists constantly. Look at your projects list as
well as your daily list at least at the beginning and the
end of each day, probably more often. Reexamine your
priorities at the beginning of a new day—you may see
things in a different light. Don't get bogged down with
nonessentials.
• At the end of the day, think about tomorrow and rewrite
your daily list, with your major priorities on top. This is
the time to consolidate the little scraps of paper with
"Call Jack at Perfect Products" that you've scratched
down in the course of the day.

Don't let your list get out of hand. If your projects or daily list has so many items that you need an index to find something, then the point has been lost. Stick to one page!

People have very different methods when it comes to the practical "school supplies" aspect of list-keeping. Some will use any scrap of paper or any stub of pencil that is lying around. Others cannot organize their thoughts without a fine-nib fountain pen and pads of paper with a high rag content with the list-maker's name artistically arranged on top.

- Use the same sort of paper for all your lists. You'll then be able to pick them out easily from your other papers. Choose a color—something that shouts "I am a list" at your unconscious.
- Try legal pads, or small pads of paper supplied by your office. Index cards don't crumple easily and can be stored in boxes. Little spiral-bound notebooks are good because you can tear out the pages as your tasks are completed (or keep them for a record).

Many experienced list-makers hail those stick-on slips that come in different pastel shades. Keep a list of a month's activities on the right side of a piece of legal paper, and write your daily list on stick-on slips attached to the left side. When a job is done, the slip is thrown away and becomes history! A perfect day is one in which the left side of the paper is completely blank and ready for the next day's set of stick-ons.

APPOINTMENT BOOKS AND CALENDARS

Lists are not the only time-planning tools that you use every day. Most people use them in combination with an appointment book, scheduling chart, or calendar.

Diaries and calendars have two main functions. They can tell you where you *will* be, and they can tell you where you *have* been and what you've done—helpful information if you're trying to see where time has been wasted or used inefficiently or to pat yourself on the back for a productive week or year.

There are many different kinds of appointment books, logs, calendars, scheduling aids. You can buy leather-bound books with a page for every day and the gross national product of every country listed in the back, as well as the birthstone for each date and the national flower for every state. You can get spiral-bound notebooks, paper-bound books, calendars published by banks and shoe repair shops—there is even a battery-operated wall calendar that lights up to remind you of important dates. Computer programs to organize your day, month, and year are available.

In other words, you certainly can find a time-planner that is visually and spatially pleasing to you, but what do you do with it?

- If you want a great deal of guidance from your appointment book, choose a total organizer like the Filofax. These are pocket-sized loose-leaf books that you can customize to your own needs.

  No part of your life is left unplanned with these. You can buy preprinted notebook pages that cover investments, business expenses, daily, weekly, and monthly

schedules, projects, shopping lists, hotel addresses, an
auto log, personal contacts, personal services—you get
the idea. You can even buy a contents page so that you
don't get lost in your own planner.

- Whatever sort of book you choose, make sure that both
business and personal appointments are noted. Your
two lives overlap, and you will certainly need to make
business appointments while at home and tennis dates at
the office.

- Put down all firm commitments at the beginning of the
year—vacations, weddings, children's birthdays, sales
conferences. It's best to know as soon as possible—and
will save a lot of rescheduling and wasted time later—if
your sister's wedding is going to conflict with a major
business presentation.

- Make a copy of your appointment book from time to
time. If you ever lose it, you will not want to spend the
time to reconstruct every future appointment. A quick
Xerox of the rest of the year might save you enormous
headaches, or keep a duplicate on a desk calendar or on
your computer.

- Be sure you indicate where and what. Be specific when
you enter an appointment on your calendar. The word
"meeting" will mean little when you encounter it in three
months.

The classic mistake: Nancy and Joy are sitting in their
respective offices making lunch plans for July 23.
Nancy mutters as she writes, "Lunch with Joy ...
12:30." Joy flips to July 23 and writes, "Lunch ...
12:30." Come July 23, will Joy remember with whom
she should lunch?

- Keep materials related to each scheduled appointment together for easy referral—a list of conference participants, for example, might be kept in the same file as a copy of your completed and rehearsed presentation for that conference, along with travel directions.
- Mark the current date in your pocket diary for instant access. Use paper clips or rubber bands to follow your progress through the month, or cut off the bottom corner of the previous days. Figure out a system so you don't waste time thumbing through the pages. (Day Runners even have a movable plastic insert marked "Today"!)
- Share your schedule with your co-workers. A wall calendar or chart showing project progress or schedules is the easiest method. Be sure you (or your husband) can be reached by phone at all times, in case of emergency.
- Use your appointment diaries and calendars to figure out where time is being wasted. For a month, keep a careful record—with your diary as your guide—of exactly how much time is being spent on each activity. Do afternoon meetings tend to drag on until quitting time? Is your boss always an hour late for your regular weekly meeting? Do you postpone your checkup every month because you're too busy? Be realistic, based on experience!
- Learn to say no. As your calendar fills up with meetings, lunch dates, and more meetings, reconsider your priorities. Don't go unless you really need to gather information or make an appearance. Send a deputy if you can. Be politic, but use your best judgment to try to cut down on time wasters.

ORGANIZATION TOOLS

Take advantage of the tools available to get organized.

- The Rolodex system is an ideal replacement for a phone book, especially if many people need to access it, there are frequent changes and additions, or your writing is so messy that only typed addresses and phone numbers will do.
- Attach business cards directly to your Rolodex. On the back, jot down whatever you want to remember and tape across the top of the Rolodex card so that you can have access to the information on the back.
- Regularly weed out your Rolodex, but keep discarded cards in the back of your files for a few years. You never know when you might need them.
- Get the most out of your Rolodex by using different-colored Rolodex cards for quick reference. You can then pick out personal, business, and client phone numbers quickly. Put frequently called numbers inside a colored plastic sleeve, which protects the card and makes it readily visible.
- If you need to keep a lot of information on clients, use a large-size card, three-by-five or six-by-nine, to set up your phone file. Note key information on each card: secretary's name, anything about the client that you'll want to bring up in conversation.
- Highlight frequently called numbers in your telephone directory. You'll be surprised how much time you save by not searching up and down the columns.
- Scheduling boards—magnetic or erasable—are great helps in depicting the flow of projects and people. The

time and expense entailed may be more than compensated by the value of seeing the schedule before you.

- A "Do Not Disturb" sign can be a real timesaver if you
  are plagued by interruptions and have no one available
  to screen your visitors. Humorous but to-the-point signs
  are available at office supply stores.
- Personal computers are the newest organizational tool.
  The avant-garde never handle a piece of paper—no
  lists, no appointment books, no charts. It's all in their
  laptops!

WORK SPACE

Arrange your work space to be as comfortable and efficient
as possible.

- Good lighting is essential. If all you have are a few
  fluorescent lights in your ceiling, lobby for a good desk
  lamp with diffuse, nonharsh light.
- Your chair should be comfortable but firm. You're in it a
  lot, and don't want to develop back problems. Some
  employees have been known to buy their own.
- You need enough storage space so that files don't spill
  over onto windowsills. A desk with a file drawer helps
  ensure that current files are right there when you're on
  the phone.
- Place your office equipment according to the natural
  movements of your right- or left-handedness. If you're
  right-handed, terminals, keyboards, and recording
  devices will be easier to use if they're on your right; the
  telephone belongs on the left, so you can write messages
  as you speak.

OFFICE TECHNOLOGY

Businesses are experimenting with a smorgasbord of computer-based innovations. The myriad of options is growing as computer companies vie for greater market share. Here are some tips for dealing with the technological revolutions:

• Learn to use whatever equipment your company has invested in. If your company doesn't offer a training course in computers, consider making the investment on your own. It's the "continuing education" for this decade.

• Periodically pick up a computer magazine to learn what the latest technology offers. An annual trip to a computer show will let you see the alternatives before you buy.

• Your office computer should be compatible with your home computer—ideally, an identical system. If you use your computer a good deal, maybe your company will pick up all or part of the cost of your home computer. Learn about software alternatives and how they can help in your work.

• Desk-top publishing can be a real timesaver. If you have anything to do with publications—whether books, magazines, or a company newsletter—there are programs that help you set type and format pages with text and graphics. Printers give you camera-ready copy. If your company has offset printing capability, you can do a promotion brochure in just one day.

• If your firm has standardized on one word processing program, use it. Otherwise, select a proven industry standard like WordPerfect or WordStar. Of course, your word processing package must be the same at home and at the office. You don't want to have to think, "Which system am I using?" as you work.

- Software programs encompass everything from spread-sheets to stock market analysis, graphics to accounting programs, project planning to record-keeping to a dog-training game called Puppy Love!
- Your company probably has a software expert on staff who could advise you on which programs would make *your* job easier. If not, salespeople in computer stores are very knowledgeable.

Larger corporations, or companies that are sophisticated technologically, now have electronic mail capabilities. With the proper software, you can access another computer in your network to leave messages, reports, or correspondence. Communication can be coded for the eyes of one person only, or the whole team.

If you deal with your corporation's branch in Singapore, for instance, you could use electronic mail to bypass the traditional mail delivery system entirely. When you arrive at your office in the morning, correspondence from Singapore will be in your computer system, waiting to be called up. Before you leave at night, you can respond by typing the requested information into your computer, making it avail-able to your colleagues half a world away when they arrive for work. Some tips on using E-mail:

- If your company uses E-mail internally, be sure that you have the correct software so you can participate. You don't want to be left out of the inner communications circle.
- Use the visibility E-mail provides. Particularly if you write well, make use of your computer for maximum exposure. Co-workers often pay careful attention to an

electronic message, while your written memo might be
tossed out with just a glance.

- Share information and solicit opinions from employees
at all levels using the electronic mail system. The seem-
ing anonymity often encourages straight talk.

- Don't shoot off your "electronic mouth" without thinking. Just because the message disappears from your
screen doesn't mean that the words have been erased.
Contemplate all consequences before you start to type.

- Do you have a document with text or illustrations that
you must send immediately to a co-worker in Montana?
If you both have facsimile (fax) machines, you can use
your equipment to send a copy of any document in as
little as fifteen seconds. A fax machine is about the size
of a small copier and operates by using telephone lines.
You only have to place the call!

Other electronic tools can help you work more efficiently
and professionally.

- An electronic whiteboard helps if you have a lot of
meetings at which you need to draw diagrams or outline
ideas. The board is used like a chalkboard. When you
roll back a completed section, the machine reduces the
material and duplicates it on an $8^1/_2$-by-11 sheet, with
suitable resolution for Xeroxing. Your complicated budget can be reduced and copied for the meeting participants in minutes!

- Video has become a necessity in some fields: advertising, casting offices, marketing, anything to do with the
theater, TV, film. Companies and institutions now make
their own videos, whether for advertising, for in-house
training, or for dissemination of information to employees.

- The typewriter has not been completely superseded. Many companies still prefer a simple typewriter for typing labels and envelopes. There exist now electronic typewriters that buzz if you've made a spelling error, have extensive memories, can erase whole lines quickly, and in some cases function as a simple word processor. One of these may have the capabilities that you need.

Other inventions are just waiting to be introduced into common use. It may turn out that office workers will not have to dream up ways to cut down on paper; in time, new machinery may exile every sheet to obsolescence. In the meantime, a key to timesaving will be handling the paper flow.

CHAPTER THREE

Handling Paper Flow

"Paperwork costs American business more than $100 billion a year," says Margaret Magnus in *The New York Times.* "For every dollar the companies spend to print forms, they spend $20 to $80 to process, copy, distribute and destroy them."

It is not surprising to learn that computer companies are on the leading edge of the attempt to cut the deluge of paper down to manageable size. But, for now, you still get a lot of paper dumped on your desk each morning, and a lot of time is wasted each day as you process it. There *are* some techniques to help you make short work of that pile.

- When you pick up a piece of paper, do something with it. Avoid the directionless shifting of papers from pile to pile in an orgy of rearranging. Keep your timesaving goal firmly in mind: you want to move each memo, report, or letter off your desk and on its way as soon as possible. Deal with each paper only once!
- Keep the decks clear. Unless you actually are inspired creatively by piles of paper, stacks of magazines, and the general welter of old files, neatness probably *does* count.

Only material relevant to the day's work should be in evidence. Behind the closed drawers of your file cabinets, all should be in order. You will get through your day's work faster if the files that you need are where they should be.

• Don't be fooled by stereotypes! When the movies or TV depicts a business person, it's usually in an immense office with a battery of phones on a designer desk with not a paper, paper clip, or roll of Scotch tape in sight. Do not emulate this image—you are never too grand to have your own office supplies, and you'll save a lot of time if you don't have to get up from your desk to ask for supplies.

MAIL

• Who should open the mail? You may want to do it yourself, to keep in touch with what's coming into the office on a daily basis. A glance at trade journals, junk mail, even job applications, may help you to keep up with trends in your field.

• Don't read junk mail unless you're in a highly technical field and really need to see equipment offerings—in which case, it's not junk. If you have an assistant, let him or her sort the mail first and pass along anything that looks useful.

• Given the trend for some important mail to look like junk mail, someone should at least *open* each envelope. A quick glance should sort the good from the bad.

• It's a great time-waster to have to explain every chore to an assistant as you process the mail. It may be quicker to pop a note into an envelope yourself or cut out a clip-

ping from a newspaper and route it to a superior. Learn
to do things on your own if it will save time. (This does
not mean packing four thousand advertising brochures
into cartons—unless this happens to be part of your
job. See the section on delegating in chapter 4.)

- When you take a business trip, pack some envelopes,
  mailing labels, and filled-out Express Mail forms so you
  can send something back to the office ASAP.

- Learn to read quickly, even if it means taking a speed-
  reading course. The purpose of speed-reading is not to
  zip through *Hamlet*, Elizabeth Barrett Browning, or the
  Bible in forty-five minutes. But much of the printed
  material that crosses your desk cries out to be skimmed
  and then disposed of. Learn to extract the necessary
  kernel from written material and pass lightly over the
  rest.

- Place articles and reports that require more time in your
  briefcase for study while you commute, get your hair
  cut, or wait in line at the bank.

- Don't let unread newspapers, journals, and reports pile
  up. After a while, you won't even see them. If a couple of
  months have passed and you haven't gotten to them,
  take an hour and clip important articles to be read at a
  later date. If you have an assistant, that person could
  take care of this chore.

- Each year, review your subscriptions at home and work.
  Do you really need each one? If you're not sure, skip it
  for a few months and see if you miss it.

- Cultivate the techniques of old-fashioned concentration.
  Do not go through the paperwork that faces you in the
  morning until you're feeling reasonably awake and can
  really *see* what you're looking at. If you are still fuzzy,
  you will either make mistakes or not absorb what you're
  reading.

- You can teach yourself to focus, even if you're tired. Force yourself to think only one thought at a time until you come to a decision.

RESPONSE TO THE WRITTEN WORD

The march of paper across your desk has a cause-and-effect dynamic. You send out reports, memos, letters, and others respond. You *get* reports, memos, letters, and have to do something about them. To do all your paperwork chores as quickly as possible, apply "minimalist" techniques when a response is necessary. Make a call if a note is not needed; a note in lieu of a memo; a memo in place of a report.

- In some situations, you can write your answer on the memo or report itself. Your response will show that you read it, heeded it, and you didn't need to keep it. It's back on the sender's desk! (You might have to keep a copy for your files.)
- If you're sending thanks for a job well done or a favor performed, congratulations to a colleague on a promotion or a new baby or a good idea, do it immediately. A few handwritten sentences on your office stationery or personal writing paper will be enough, or a phone call may be sufficient. But remember: it might be quicker to jot a note to someone than to spend half a day playing telephone tag. A rule of thumb: If you can't get hold of your target on the first phone call, send a note.
- Adjust your standards of perfection to the situation at hand. Consider your audience. You're writing a letter or memo to a supplier that you contact once a week? It

truly won't matter if a word has been left out—don't waste time in redoing it. Write it in with a pen, and send the letter on its way. On the other hand, a résumé, job application, final report, or anything written for the signature of others must be perfect.

- If your handwriting is not legible, type a brief answer and staple it to the original letter or memo. Return both to the sender.

- Your responses, simple though they might be, may have to be copied and filed, but that takes a lot less time than dictating a formal letter or typing a perfect reply yourself.

- Don't forget carbon paper, it's making a comeback! There are all kinds of memos on the market that come with their own carbon and second sheet. They're perfect for short notes.

- If your response memos often say the same thing, think about preprinted forms—write a few basic samples that will cover most situations and use them whenever possible.

A New York City gynecologist always sent a handwritten note to his patients when the examination tests came back, in most cases saying that all was fine and that there was nothing to worry about. One patient came across the doctor's note from the previous year in her files and noticed that it was exactly like the just-received message from her most recent visit—identical in spacing and phrasing and letter formation. Upon examination, she found that the enterprising physician had hand-written an original—probably ten years before—and then had it printed. She couldn't have cared less—she was delighted that her health was okay!

- Respond to letters and memos promptly, even if caught in a terrible time crunch. Avoid the remind memo from your boss wondering if you had any ide on the problem that he described in his memo of two weeks ago. And don't be the last person to congratulate a colleague or react to a report. Correspondence with clients and suppliers should obviously be kept up to the minute—after all, that's your *job*.
- If you've been on vacation, determine what letters and memos shouldn't be answered at all. It's no use coming up with a solution to a problem that was forgotten ten days before.

PAPER MANAGEMENT

Do you have the sort of job in which you concentrate on one project at a time (for example, an entry-level electrical engineer)? Do you have several areas of responsibility (such as an editor at a monthly magazine), or have so many unrelated professional chores to tackle at once that you need computer help to keep it all straight (general manager of a discount clothing chain)? The more diffused your job, the more you need a convenient, predetermined place for every item or category of paper that crosses your desk. On the first pass at your paperwork, make sure that each piece is moved farther along the chain to final processing.

- Be ruthless with things like sales reports. If they're not vital to your job, throw them out. You can always get another copy if needed.
- Have a special file for information that will be needed for only a few days: a program for a business lunch, for example, or your boss's travel itinerary. Go through

the file once a week and throw out everything whose moment has passed.
- Someone else's desk might be the best place for a paper that came to your desk first. Reroute it. If the outcome of the job is something that you need to know about, make a note to yourself to check up on it.
- Have an "in process" box, into which you put anything current that is applicable to that day's work. If you have to deal with a series of files at once, or piles of paper on a particular topic, get a "to do" table—one long enough to hold all the necessary files or papers.
- There are some papers that you have to keep—important letters, technical information, project background data that you will need again. If one of these items requires no further action at the moment, file it and be sure to date it—this will aid you immeasurably in keeping your files current.
- Before you start work, glance at everything in your paperwork pile just so that there are no unpleasant surprises.

One middle manager was sent by his company to an intensive weekend seminar to hone his management skills.

The weekend started badly when he solved his first problem incorrectly. He was presented with a full in-box and given an hour to deal with it as he normally would. He started at the top of the pile, and went through the papers in the box one by one. He wrote answers to letters and memos, made decisions, threw out irrelevant material. Unfortunately, when he reached the bottom of the pile, he discovered a memo that contained information that completely negated everything he had done during the exercise.

- You may need to take work with you when you're a\
from the office, to do at home, while traveling or waitin\
at the dentist's. Be sure your briefcase has the necessary
supplies. A calculator? A pencil? Legal pads? Be prepared.
- Wage a campaign of your own against all that paperwork. If you're in a supervisory position, make it clear
that a six-page memo doesn't interest you—one page
will do.
- Don't ask a secretary to make an extra copy of a report
"just in case we need it." Wait until you need it, if *ever!*
- When you're routed some in-house information that you
always throw out, you might go to the source and see if
your name could be removed from the distribution list.
But be tactful. If you know that a particular report is
someone's pride and joy, let it go even if you never look
at it.

FILING SYSTEMS

The point of keeping files is to be able to retrieve useful
information. If the information that you've carefully put
away is not useful, or if you cannot find it, then your whole
system needs rethinking. A few basics apply to most situations:

- Set up your own files. You may not be responsible for
keeping them up to date on a daily basis, but make sure
that as the system matures, you continue to understand
it. Your secretary may move on, and *you* will have to train
the new one. You will also have to find information in
your files yourself at times. Even if you have an entire

office staff, you may be on your own in the evenings or on weekends. Don't waste time by not knowing exactly where to look.

- If most of your company's data are filed on computer disks, become computer literate so you can retrieve information quickly and easily. In the long run, it is professional suicide to be unfamiliar with any of the relevant technology in your office. Even if you have to *pay* an expert to stay with you after hours to teach you, learn it!

- When you name your files, avoid flights of fancy and associations known only to you. Your logic will not necessarily seem crystal-clear to someone else. Make your filing categories broad. If they are very specialized, you will have too many files and problems finding anything.

- When you label individual file folders, use nouns as the first word, then a qualifying noun or adjective. For example: "Tax Forms—Corporate" and "Tax Forms—Individual."

- Consult with co-workers who are most likely to be using the files also. Establish which common nouns come most easily to mind for the majority on any hard-to-identify project.

- Cross-reference. If one might logically look in two places for a file, choose the name that comes first alphabetically and cross-reference the other.

- All papers should be filed facing the same way for quick reference. Date and staple everything. No paper clips that will come off and fall to the bottom of the file. File chronologically, last in front, *every time*.

- Thin your files regularly. It's generally easiest to review a few files a week. Keep a colored marker in the file cabinet showing where you left off last time. When you get to the end, it will probably be time to start again!

- Keep active files handy. It's a waste of time for you to get

up from your desk to consult a file that you might use
ten times a day. Have a spacious file drawer either in
your desk or within reaching distance. Be sure to review
the contents of the drawer regularly.

- Index or summarize the contents of a file on the cover if
you have overstuffed files, and you can't break them
down into further categories. The searcher then can tell
quickly what's inside without thumbing through a hundred sheets. Or use loose-leaf binders with dividers for
thick, unwieldy files.

- If you need to keep background research material—
articles from magazines and newspapers that you have

Be sensible about handling materials that are not
pieces of paper that fit easily into file cabinets, such as
microfilm, videotapes, outsize photographs, or artwork
that is pasted down on large boards. These objects are
fragile and should not be pawed over every time you
look for an item. Each item should be:

- Wrapped in something dustproof like heavy brown
wrapping paper.
- Marked with a number and description of everything that is in the package.
- Entered—with the number and the description—
in a notebook or file folder or index card, or put on
your computer. This should tell where the item is
stored.

This procedure will save time and hysteria the next
time someone looks for the photograph of the CEO
that appeared in last year's annual report. Annotated
indexes are time-consuming to set up, but you will gain
a dividend of more time eventually saved.

to refer to—don't overclip. Keep only those articles that
would be hard to find again—from a foreign-language
journal, for example. Don't stuff your files with articles
that can easily be resurrected from the library or your
company's on-line computer.

- Keep an index of the articles that interest you. List the
name and date of the periodical and what the article was
about. It takes up a lot less space than trying to file bulky
clippings.

- Do not keep anything valuable in your files—something
that would cause great inconvenience or financial loss if
it were stolen or damaged by fire (financial instruments,
corporate papers, classified plans). These items belong
in a company safe or a secured, fireproof facility. If you
must keep important personal papers in your office, be
sure that they're kept in a separate, locked drawer. Of
course, personnel papers—salary information and performance reviews—should also be secure.

MEMOS

Before you start any written project, ask yourself if the letter,
report, or memo *needs* to be written. Is it important that
there be a record? Will a short memo be a timesaver if
someone is not available?

If you decide that it's *not* necessary to go through the
writing, editing, and distribution process, that the written
item will neither help you professionally nor speed along the
work of your department, skip it! Make a phone call or have
a brief meeting.

Even if you are wedded to the idea of cutting down on the
excessive flow of paperwork, there will be times when you
have to write something. Positions sometimes have to be

stated formally in a work situation; information has to be shared; office dynamics indicate that putting a thought or criticism in writing is the best idea. Your goal is to produce the written word as economically as possible, wasting minimal time—both yours and the readers'.

- Never underestimate the power of the file memo. You may think that you will remember the details of a conversation or meeting but a lot may intervene before you need to recall it. Write down the details in a file memo— just a few lines are enough—and if a decision is reviewed, you will have the documentation.

A rule of thumb when deciding whether or not to write a memo. If there is no need for your memo to live forever in someone's file, or if your memo is likely to beget other memos, pick up the phone and get the problem solved. Document the exchange with a file memo, if necessary.

- An emotional time-saver: If you fly into a rage about something, and feel compelled to put it all down on paper, with the original memo to the villain who crossed you and carbons to everyone from the president to your spouse, wait at least twenty-four hours before you write a word. You may feel different tomorrow.

REPORTS

- If you have a lengthy report to prepare, treat it as you would any other project. Make a schedule. You might, for example, plan on completing a rough draft on Tuesday evening, and editing and polishing it on Wednesday.

- Give yourself a rather tight schedule and don't allow yourself to relax. Your mind will wander.
- If you are not used to writing, do an outline first, noting the points that you want to cover. That ought to get you started.
- Take your outline and start to write. Do not linger, searching for the perfect word. Don't take too much time with the introduction on your first draft. As the report evolves, you might find that your perspective changes a little, so a new introduction may be necessary. A word processor is a great help in spontaneous writing, since making changes is so simple.

Take advantage of word processing systems. If your office remains in the backwaters of yesterday, or if you're a free-lance writer who still hunts and pecks on the old IBM electric, investigate the joys of word processing:

- Retyping is eliminated. Your work, stored on disks, can be displayed on a screen at any time to review, make editorial changes, and correct mistakes. When your latest version is ready, print it out as "hard copy."
- Co-workers with compatible systems can take your disk and work on it at their own terminals. Local area networks allow many people to share work and information. Multiple input is possible with minimum effort.
- Updating material is easy. Disks can be stored until a future date—then new material can be added in a few minutes and hard copy printed out if necessary.

- Learn to write clearly and concisely. Les.
  Remember that you're engaged in business wr.
  your freshman composition class at college.
- Be as brief as possible. Look at your first and last
  graphs especially and shorten them if possible. T. .e
  are often vague introductions and summations and
  sometimes can be cut out entirely. If your report is very
  long, or very complicated, it will be a service to your
  reader to begin with a summary.
- Don't forget to edit. Be ruthless. As you review your
  work, cut anything that is not absolutely necessary. If
  you have a lot of technical data to support your points,
  they belong in an appendix—or in your office files,
  available upon request.

WORKING WITH A SECRETARY OR ASSISTANT

Do you have a secretary who takes dictation? If so, do you
know how to dictate? This is a skill not everyone develops
naturally.

- Think through what you want to say at the beginning so
  that you won't need to correct yourself mid-thought.
- Make notes so that you don't forget any points.
- Speak slowly.
- Spell out proper names and any technical terms.
- Indicate punctuation.
- Use a dictaphone to answer letters or do your own corre-
  spondence in airports, taxis, or when you're stuck at
  home with a fever.
- If you have a very good secretary or assistant, he or she
  may be able to draft much of your correspondence. As

he gets used to your ways and to your writing style, and learns about clients and office personnel, a short note indicating along what lines you want correspondence answered or report written may suffice.

* Hire the best secretary or assistant you can afford. This will probably turn out to be your biggest timesaver of all.
* If you hire college interns, learn to make good use of their time. Let them work on a free-standing project that requires research and is not dependent on day-to-day knowledge of your company. Give them an outline, some idea of what your conclusions will probably be, and clues as to where the supporting data might be found. Let them do the writing.

DISTRIBUTION

* Does everyone who gets written material that originates from your office really need it? Or want it? Check twice a year. When you send out regular memos or reports to a distribution list, periodically attach a slip asking if the recipient wants to be retained on that list. Cull those who do not respond. Don't be guilty of adding unwanted paper.
* Don't be afraid to question distribution tradition. It may be that your department has *always* sent out weekly sales figures to just about everyone, dating from the days when there were fifteen employees and everyone was involved in most aspects of company management. Now there are six hundred employees, and you suspect that if anyone really needs the sales figures, they can call and ask for a copy. Check with your supervisor to see if this particular time-waster could be eliminated.

CHAPTER FOUR

Managing at Work

PERSONNEL MANAGEMENT

Successful staff management establishes a win-win situation in a department. Your team learns efficient ways, and if they perform, they prosper. You, the manager, have a reliable staff that you can count on—and they help make you a fast-tracker in the eyes of top management.

The basic rule to developing a good team: hire the very best people you can find. This holds true at every level, from beginning secretary to department head.

As you build the best team available, your basic management strategy is to invest time to save time. With competent, well-trained staff, projects get done more efficiently, faster, and your department works together for the best result.

You probably know what you expect from your staff—loyalty, hard work, attention to detail, creative problem-solving, a certain amount of goodwill and flexibility in a work situation. But what should they expect of you? Set guidelines to provide the kind of good management needed in the give-and-take of office dynamics.

Be civil. Try not to react to occasional hostility. As a woman, you have probably already discovered that some men have a problem working for you. You also will have learned that some *women* have trouble working for you—they were brought up to see men as the authority figures. Do not try to fit yourself into a mold that is not natural to you—you don't have to be one of the boys. Just let time and results prove that you are as capable of being in charge as anyone.

- There is a tradition among men in American business that tough is best. If this is not your personality, don't bother to emulate it: you'll just put people off. You can achieve as much by always being polite; request, don't demand. The autocratic command is going out of fashion in today's corporate culture.
- Remain available to your superiors and your staff. Don't get an upset stomach every time the phone rings or someone knocks on your door and your schedule is disrupted once again.
- Keep in close contact with your office colleagues. Build unplanned time into your daily schedule to get to know the people you're working with, as well as your clients and suppliers. If you don't, you won't be able to tell what your boss or client really wants, or what your staff is actually capable of.
- Be sensitive to the needs of your staff. You will understand their strengths and weaknesses better and be more in tune with office dynamics.
- Listen to your staff. Find out what they think is good, and bad, about each job situation. Try to help.
- Give advice carefully and thoughtfully. Your staff will be very interested in what you think, because you hold the current key to their further advancement. Don't abuse or make light of this power.
- Try to be flexible. Be sympathetic to the many working

parents in the workforce these days. They need al. help they can get in dealing with backbreaking schedules and multiple responsibilities.

- You are the manager, and job performance does come first. With that understood, suggesting a day off here or there for an overworked employee does no harm, and may be quite meaningful in the life of the staff member.
- Do not become a best friend of your employee. Try to strike a balance with your staff—you are the boss, yet you continue to show friendly interest. If you try to keep your people happy, they will reward you with better job performance.
- Be clear when instructing your staff. Never assume that the ins and outs of an assignment are automatically understood by all, and that your priorities are obvious to your employees. Especially when dealing with new hires, explain and explain again.
- Make sure your employees make your load easier. Invest training time in the beginning to save time later. But the training period cannot go on endlessly. The new employee must start to make independent decisions early on.
- If a new hire turns out not to be a team player, and if you need cooperation to function well, let the person know right away that he or she is not working out and should start to look for a new position. Don't prolong the decision beyond a reasonable trial period.
- You have the right to take your team's loyalty for granted. If you manage well, your employees' self-interest will be congruent with that of the firm's in most cases. As long as your staff is working for you, and being paid by your company, you can expect them to generally put their employer's interests first. Those who always put their needs ahead of the corporation's should be let go.

DELEGATING

The job of a manager is to manage. That means that whatever the function of your department, it is your responsibility to see that the assignments are carried out efficiently,
on time, and with a minimum of fuss. You cannot do everything yourself.

You need help, which was the point of hiring the best staff
possible. Now that you've got them, use them! You must give
up some of your duties and learn to delegate properly. Most
experts feel that this ability is the most important of all
managerial functions.

- Don't be afraid to assign tedious, repetitive work to your
  staff. You had to do chores on your way up—you still do,
  and so do they. If you have a prince or princess who is
  not willing to share the load of tedium, let them try their
  luck at another company. If you are too diffident to
  assign unpleasant tasks—you want to be loved, and you
  want your staff to have *fun*—your employees will be
  doing the creative research and you will be entering
  data on charts. Let them aspire to reach your level so
  they won't have to do the drudgery anymore.
- Hard, boring work does deserve a reward. Try to
  include in your staff's assignments some challenging,
  interesting tasks as well.
- Don't be arrogant. Even when you think, "I can do this
  better and faster than anyone else," you must avoid the
  temptation to do so. If you do, you will be wasting your
  staff's time, and your company's money, and probably
  stressing yourself to the limit. Maybe you *can* do a task
  better and faster, but that doesn't mean that your assistant can't do it well enough; in time, she will be better

and faster, too. Give your staff room to grow. And give yourself a break.

- Don't fear losing control. An inability to let go lies at the bottom of many troubled managers' avoidance of true delegation. Control of every detail is not what you are there for. You were hired to build a competent team, each of whom has an important function. Your staff members are not meant to be the reflection of your glory—they are meant to do a great deal of the work. If you are taking care of every single detail, you are also losing sight of the big picture.

- Don't underrate your staff. You must really believe that each one is capable of doing an excellent job (although some will have strengths that others do not have) or you will not have the confidence to give them an assignment and let them carry it forward on their own. They will learn only by doing.

- Set definite deadlines for each assignment you delegate. Do not assume that all is going smoothly as the weeks go by. Interim progress reports are a help to you and your staff.

- Think out and communicate the reason for each deadline; your employee should know which deadlines have some leeway and which are a matter of financial life or death. Profit goes out the window if a consumer magazine is even a day late on the newsstands, for example. If a prototype of your product must be ready on a certain day because it's being flown to China on a chartered jet, make sure your staff knows all the details.

- Don't inadvertently set your staff up for failure. Use common sense when you give an assignment. Make sure that your staff member has the background and expertise to really do the job. If you're in doubt, make the task a team assignment. Match two complementary employees, each with a different strength.

- Make sure when you delegate a project—perhaps one that was handled by you in the past—that your team member has the authority to implement the job. This may involve phone calls from you, making sure others understand that this person is your deputy and you expect him or her to be aided accordingly.
- You can never explain too much, especially with new staff. If you have assigned a complicated, multistaged undertaking, discuss details. If part of the project is due by a certain date, make sure your employee understands. You should receive detailed progress reports.
- Even though you keep an eye on all projects being handled by your staff, that does not mean that you expect to find the job back on your desk before it's completed. You must make it clear when you delegate authority that you're delegating responsibility as well. When the going gets tough, you're available for consultation, but you expect your assistant to do the job.
- Your staff must understand not only the project but also how it fits into the bigger picture in your company. Be sure you discuss sufficiently the point of the endeavor. Share information. If the thrust changes, let the staff know.
- When the project is completed, offer both well-meant criticism and well-deserved praise for a job well done. You will never build a loyal staff unless they feel that you appreciate their efforts and evaluate those efforts realistically.
- If you have to find fault, try to combine the bad with some good to remove the sting. Your best management approach to correction is a straightforward we're-all-in-this-together and a sense of partnership in improving problem-solving skills.
- When you are criticized by your boss, try not to take it personally. Learn from justifiable criticism. If you can

see yourself as management sees you, it's possible that you can evaluate your own job performance and improve it.

(For practical advice on managing criticism and making it a positive experience, see *Criticism in Your Life: How to Give It, How to Take It, How to Make It Work for You,* by Dr. Deborah Bright [New York: MasterMedia Limited, 1988].)

- See any project through to the end. You may need to follow up with top management on your report or find out how a new line of children's pajamas is doing in the Midwest or whether your team's method of teaching Japanese really works. Corporate loyalty and identity stem from the ability of a management team to see how their work actually affects their company's efficiency, bottom line, or corporate image.

As manager, there are some aspects of your position that you should never delegate. These are the tasks that are inherent to your position. It would be inappropriate for anyone other than yourself to take them over:

- If you are expected to appear in your official capacity as department head at any kind of corporate function, do so. It is not a good idea to have your assistant appear in your place at a company picnic, large meeting, sales conference, or the meet-and-greet tea with new clients.
- *You* deal with your personnel. You hire, fire, and give raises. You explain *why* to employees who are not going to get bonuses this year. You must not delegate this responsibility, even though it's never pleasant to tell a perfectly good employee that her job is being terminated because of a budget cut.
- You take ultimate responsibility for everything that hap-

pens in your department. If one of your staff has com-
mitted a really awful mistake—through inattention has
bought 400,000 pencils instead of 400—you must be in
the front line enduring the heat. You may ultimately fire
that person, but you're the one who should face top
management.

- If you have a secretary, in addition to a staff of non-
  secretarial employees, don't forget him or her. Like all
  your other employees, you have hired the best person
  you could find. Use this person to capacity, give as much
  responsibility as possible, and hand off as much routine
  management as is feasible. Responsibility can help
  develop more creative, more dedicated employees.
- You may find a truly devoted staff member in your
  secretary, who is more involved with, and more knowledgeable about, the details of your life than any of your
  other employees. Make it worthwhile for this person to
  take some initiative. It will save you time. Give credit
  when it's due. Your secretary makes it possible for you to
  shine. Acknowledge this help often and sincerely.
- Respect the person who has chosen to take a job as
  secretary rather than attempting to move up the ladder
  in other professional areas. This person surely has other
  priorities—family, personal, or educational—that make
  a job with regular hours and steady pay right for them.

FREE-LANCERS

Timesavers that hardly ever get mentioned are those almost
invisible employees, the consultants and free-lancers of all
stripes.

With corporate layoffs, cutbacks, and mergers, there are a
lot of experts available for consulting assignments who have

decided that they would rather take a chance on their own business abilities than rely on others. Hence you can easily find the services of writers, researchers, engineers, management consultants, caterers, artists. . . . If you find that you're completely overwhelmed seasonally, why not give your staff a break and bring in some outside help until the pace slows?

It *is* hard to work free-lancers into the general fabric of day-to-day office life. They don't know anyone, they don't understand the corporate culture, and you don't want to waste time training someone who will be there for a month. It's your job to make best use of free-lancers.

- Select a project that an outsider can do easily—a computer program that needs to be improved, or a line of costume jewelry to be designed. Match the free-lancer and the job carefully.
- Before you hire a free-lancer, try to get a reference from someone you trust. Consultants can appear with extremely impressive résumés, but the only way that you

If you are uneasy about a free-lancer's credentials, do not hire that person. A managing editor of a major New York publishing company tells of the seemingly capable free-lance copy editor who just couldn't quite get the book she had been assigned completed. Frequent phone calls over a period of a week elicited promises of "Tomorrow." Finally, the desperate managing editor sent a staff member to knock on the free-lancer's door. No response. The next day a box was delivered to the editor. In it was the manuscript—it had been shredded into tiny pieces, like confetti. Yes, there was a copy, but this was a very inefficient way to produce a book.

can really predict if a good job will be delivered on time and on budget is to talk with someone who has actually worked with the prospective free-lancer.

- Some corporations require that a contract be signed with any free-lancer, which will spell out fee and delivery date. Whether or not you use a contract, put your agreement in writing.
- Call the free-lancer mid-project to make sure that the work is on schedule and that there are no problems.
- If the free-lancers work in your office, assign a staff member to help them get their bearings. Try to find them reasonably comfortable work space. This is sometimes impossible, and they have to make do with the space of someone who is on vacation, but if the free-lancers will be with you for a while, try to find them a spot of their own.
- Don't ignore the free-lancers. Make sure they know that their work is appreciated. If you use free-lancers on a regular basis, your life will be much easier if you can establish a stable of competent helpers whom you can call on again and again.
- Pay the free-lancer on time. Many live close to the financial edge and count on receiving their checks within about three weeks. If your company has a policy of paying everybody within ninety days, either try to make special arrangements for your temporary personnel or tell the free-lancers what they can expect.

MEETINGS

Legend has it that one large corporation has a conference room with neither tables nor chairs. Meetings are short and remarkably productive. Such a revolutionary management technique, however, is not likely to become a trend, and time wasted in boring, pointless meetings will continue to be a source of complaint.

A recent survey by a New York City human resources consulting firm revealed that more than one-third of the average management employee's workday is consumed by meetings. At their worst, they're expensive time-wasters. At their best, they are effective management tools for problem-solving and promoting team spirit. Either way, they are a fact of business life and a vital part of the corporate culture through which information is transmitted up and down the ranks. They are also part of the corporate power structure through which people tend to judge their own importance, as well as the importance of others.

Whether you are the person organizing a meeting, an attendee, or a participant in a one-on-one conference, whether the goal is to share information or to solve a problem, meetings afford high visibility and give you a chance to shine before your peers and superiors. Similarly, they can provide insight into how effective your colleagues and employees are.

At issue is how to make the best of them, how to eliminate unnecessary meetings, how to keep control so they accomplish their purpose with a minimum of wasted time.

If you are responsible for holding meetings, consider the following:

- Is your regularly scheduled staff meeting really necessary? Has the list of attendees increased with time? Prune the list of participants next time or cut weekly sessions down to twice a month. You can always use the telephone or memos to stay in touch or give information.
- Conduct informal one-on-one meetings or small group meetings when possible, instead of convening the whole department. Large meetings tend to take on a life of their own and can drag on forever.

- Occasionally, a report may take the place of a meeting. This works only when you don't think that there will be questions and comments about the information you are sharing. You don't want to avoid a meeting only to encounter endless back-and-forth memo-writing.
- Put your meeting notes in a file, in case questions arise later, with a cover memo stating that a meeting was held on a certain date, attended by various staff.
- If a meeting seems like overkill, there is always a phone call. Settle the matter over the phone, then write a short file note if you think it's indicated.
- How do you keep a meeting short? Call it for 4:30 in the afternoon, and do not stray from the agenda.

Preparation

- Do your homework. Provide relevant information *before* a meeting and expect everyone to have read it. Though you may want to summarize the material at the outset, don't waste time by repeating it all at the meeting.
- If the meeting's been called to solve a problem, your memo should suggest that participants come prepared to discuss *solutions* only. You'll save lots of time by not rehashing all the issues.
- Invite only those who have something to contribute or gain from attending. Don't be afraid to let people leave early if the part of the meeting that is relevant to them is over.
- Have an agenda printed and distributed several days before the meeting, so participants have time to do *their* homework. However, an agenda distributed *at* the meeting is better than none. Agendas with time slots for each item help to keep the meeting on track. Also, they promise an on-time ending, which will be much appreciated.

- You might want to review the agenda with other staff members prior to the meeting. Objectives should be agreed on in advance and stated in the agenda or meeting memo. Prioritize your agenda so that you cover what is most important in case you run out of time. Introduce short informational material at the beginning to allow discussion time at the end.
- Place items with a strong likelihood of consensus first on the agenda. This develops a pattern of cooperation and makes the group more likely to agree when dealing with more controversial issues.

The Meeting Room

Arrive early to make sure the meeting room is set up properly. Use a checklist to ensure that you haven't forgotten anything. Consider:

- A place for coats, if attendees are coming from out of the office.
- Seating cards, if you want to control who sits next to whom.
- Name tags.
- One or more flip charts and markers or chalkboards and chalk.
- Copies of the agenda.
- Pads and pencils for note-taking.
- Handouts, if any.
- Audio-visual equipment.
- Tape-recorder, if you're taping the proceedings.
- Identification of smoking and nonsmoking sections.
- Seating—number and placement. Have you arranged the room to encourage discussion and discourage private chat?

- Food and beverages. Unless you are prepared for formal dining first, make sure food is easy to serve and handle. The eating should be finished before the meeting begins.
- Phones and rest rooms—do you know where they are?
- Room temperature and ventilation. A room that is too warm and stuffy can literally put the participants to sleep.
- Size of the meeting room. Try to get one that is larger than you need. It makes participants feel important and gives them room to spread out papers, etc. The more comfortable your group, the better your chance of running an efficient meeting with all participants paying good attention.

Managing the Meeting

- Get off to a good start. Be there first to greet people individually and make introductions.
- Have a staff member there to help arriving participants if necessary. Sometimes reservations have to be confirmed or a phone call made. You want your participants to be thinking of your meeting, not whether they're going to get on the flight to Chicago.
- Start on time. Don't wait for latecomers and never apologize for starting without them.
- Identify at the outset the purpose of the meeting, what you want to accomplish, and how long it will last.
- Set a closing time and stick to it. You might even include the closing time on your printed agenda if you have one.
- Arrange beforehand that presentations will be short, leaving most of the meeting time for discussion and problem-solving.

- If presenting results of a study or a report that has required the assistance of others, acknowledge their contribution. Publicly crediting others ensures their future participation and encourages others.
- If *you* are running the meeting, have someone else take minutes or run the tape-recorder. Leave the nuts and bolts of this chore to a staff member. You don't want to have to think about it.
- Agree in advance on the ground rules for your meeting, and make sure the participants understand them. May questions be asked during the presentation, or should they be held for the end? Will there be a break? Do they need to take notes or is the material summarized in the handouts?
- Guard against one or two people monopolizing the discussion. You cannot be rude, but you can ignore them politely when they try to edge in again; make sure that others join in by asking the more retiring attendees for an opinion.
- Always call the participants by name. If it's a large group, make sure that everyone has been clearly identified.
- Summarize the results of the meeting before disbanding. If time permits and the group is small, let each attendee offer his or her final thoughts.
- Make assignments clear—tell participants what is expected of them by the next meeting, and hold them to it.
- Conclude on time! Assign someone to alert you about ten or fifteen minutes before the meeting is scheduled to end.
- End on a positive note. Even if there are unresolved problems and you need to meet again, focus on what has been accomplished.

- If there are minutes of the meeting, distribute them as soon as possible, preferably within twenty-four hours.
- Follow up on assignments made during the meeting. Offer help if needed, but expect results on time. Even if you have given a project to someone who does not usually report to you, in this committee context you can expect the same response that you would get from one of your regular team.

Visuals

Use visuals if they tell a pictorial story that can't be told as effectively with words. Think of visuals as a thing quite separate from a string of words enlarged for the screen.

- Keep slides simple—if using text only, no more than six words to a line and six lines to a slide.
- Write or draw directly on overhead transparencies in response to audience feedback to personalize your presentation.
- Keep a slide show moving—thirty seconds per slide.
- Make copies of slides and overheads to give out so participants won't have to take extensive notes. Don't hand them out until the presentation starts or they will read the material and steal your thunder.
- Adding a second or third projector lends a dynamic quality to the presentation and helps move it along more quickly.
- Overheads have an advantage over slides by allowing you to keep the lights on and let participants take notes.
- Think videotape when you need to demonstrate how to do something in detail. It's an expensive but effective solution and makes a dynamic presentation.

Being a Participant

- If you are invited to a meeting, think twice before you accept. Is your presence necessary? Can you add anything? Can you learn anything? Is it politic to go? If the answer to all the above is no, excuse yourself. But if you *should* attend and cannot make it, send a reliable alternate. Make sure that person takes good notes or tapes the meeting.
- If you are a participant, do your homework. If you have a valid point to make, raise it as soon as you can. Try to present it as an outgrowth of the discussion to which the team contributed, not as your proprietary idea.
- If you feel you must express disagreement, be conscious of the other person's need to save face and do it with tact.

ONE-ON-ONE MEETINGS

In some companies, it's perfectly all right to thrash out policy while standing in line at the water fountain. But if your corporation is rigidly hierarchical and if such informality is *not* appropriate, have a one-on-one meeting. One-on-one meetings risk being time-wasters if they lack the up-front structure of planned group meetings. To avoid the pitfalls:

- Make sure the reason for the meeting is clear. If you have suggested the meeting with a superior, you might put your request in the form of a memo.
- Organization is key. Have your backup material with

you. Listen carefully; take notes; follow up with a memo if necessary. If it's a meeting with a subordinate, ask him or her to prepare an outline or agenda, to think through in advance all the issues to be raised.

- A one-on-one with a subordinate provides a private opportunity to openly discuss difficult problems—both corporate and personal. Use this opportunity to get to know this employee better. Hold the meeting in the subordinate's office. You will get lots of clues about that individual's work habits, likes and dislikes, even strengths and weaknesses.

- To discourage the drop-in visitor—who might have business to transact with you but might just be looking for a friendly ear—close your office door when you need to work uninterrupted. You can't do this too often if you have a staff to manage, lest you lose touch with them.

- To get rid of the unwanted visitor: alert your secretary or assistant to interrupt with a phone call. A sigh and regretful "You'll have to excuse me now. This is going to

---

If you are trying to avoid a heart-to-heart with a fellow employee, schedule him or her for about ten minutes before your lunch appointment and try the ploy described by Chase Untermeyer, assistant secretary of the navy: "LBJ used to tell of asking for a meeting with FDR on a tricky subject the president wanted to duck," said Untermeyer. "Given only fifteen minutes in the Oval Office, LBJ entered, to be greeted by FDR: 'Lyndon, Harry Hopkins has just told me the most amazing thing about Russian women. Did you know . . .' By the time the anecdote was finished, the fifteen minutes were up."

take forever and I don't want to waste your time" should work.

- Stand up politely when someone comes in and *don't sit down again.* This will prevent the other party from settling in.
- As a desperate measure, take a quick look at your watch, gather your papers, and say, "Sorry, I'm late for a meeting. Let's have lunch some time soon."
- If you must see someone who chatters on and on, go to his or her office. You're free to leave when you want.

TELEPHONES

After meetings, phone calls probably consume the greatest part of your workday. If you're in sales, they may be virtually your entire day. Both blessing and curse, the telephone has made possible immediacy of communication, yet can be endlessly frustrating when the party at the other end is continually unavailable or when you are constantly interrupted. Anyone who has gotten caught in playing "telephone tag" or finds herself unable to tackle a major project because the phone keeps ringing may rue the day Alexander Graham Bell was born.

New technologies, linking touch-tone phones and computers, may promise some relief: telephone answering machines that can be accessed from an outside phone, interactive computers, electronic mail systems, all are replacing traditional phone communication, and will help businesses and individuals handle calls more efficiently and accurately.

Though the costs of much of this technology still run quite high, prices are sure to come down as competition increases. If, for example, you run a small business, are an independent consultant, work out of your own home, you should begin to explore the telecommunication options available. Even if they're too costly for the present, in a few years you may be able to afford them. In the meantime, there are some now standard telephone options to help you make most efficient use of your telephone equipment.

- Call waiting. This is a service of the telephone company that indicates someone else is calling in while you are on the phone. Be aware, however, that the beep signaling a call waiting and the time it takes you to answer the call and get back to your original conversation might annoy some people and seem discourteous. Also, if you have call waiting (or a second line, without another person to answer it), you will be the one to pay for the return call— a problem if you do a lot of overseas business.
- Call forwarding might be useful if you're out of your office for large segments of the day. This service transfers your calls to a different number. You won't miss anything important, but the client that you're visiting may not appreciate the interruptions.
- Programmable phones. You can automatically dial frequently called numbers by pressing a single button.
- Automatic redial. Ends the frustration of constant busy signals. On some phones, this option automatically rings through and signals the caller when a busy line becomes free. It's a boon when trying to make a reservation at a busy restaurant or reach someone with a time-dated or very important message.
- Speaker phones. What they lack in privacy, they make up for in convenience by freeing hands for taking notes or allowing others in the room to participate in the conversation. Get the best quality you can afford if you use it often.
- Headsets may be a solution if you're on the phone constantly and must be able to take notes.

- Telephone intercoms use a separate internal line and enable calls to be screened and announced before being put through. While practical only in an office setting, they allow private conversation between two people within an organization that cannot be heard by the caller.
- Cellular phones. If cost is not an object and you travel or are away from a phone frequently, then a cellular phone may be for you. They are expensive to buy and run and have technological bugs that interfere with transmission as of this writing, but look for these phones to come down in cost over the next few years and for quality to improve with the application of digital technology. Hand-held models have become so portable that you can make and receive calls from a supermarket aisle, a moving bus, or an airport terminal parking lot. Some say they are indispensable when running late for an appointment, waiting in an area where there is no phone, or while traveling by car. Others find it an added intrusion in a world already overpopulated with telephones.
- Paging systems and beepers free you from being tied to a phone when you must be reachable at all times. The simplest models signal you to call an answering service when a message comes through for you; more sophisticated beepers display telephone numbers to be called.
- Answering services. If you are away from your phone a great deal, another option is to hire an answering service, either round-the-clock or during specified hours, say nine to five. To test the quality of the service, call in "blind" to your number—or, even better, to another number on the service before you hire them—and leave a message. You can check efficiency, thoroughness, and courtesy this way.
- Telephone answering machines can also answer your

calls when you're out. Much less expensive than an answering service, but without the personalized touch of a live voice. Look for one that does not limit the length of message allowed. If you use it for business and are "out in the field" a lot, select one that you can call into from an outside phone for messages.

TELEPHONE MANAGEMENT TECHNIQUES

Even the most sophisticated equipment won't do much for your telephone technique if you are not well organized. The first step is having the right tools at hand:

- Create a telephone message center both at the office and at home. Keep handy pens and pencils, notepaper, a telephone log, phone books of areas in which you do frequent business, your personal phone books or Rolodex.
- Keep a clock by the phone (even a timer if you're prone to talking too long), which can help you monitor the time.

Heed the advice of Katherine Adams, vice president of marketing at Bankers Trust: "Remember that your initial introduction is your voice. The projection of your voice is very important. You want the effect to be upbeat, and the impression you give one of authority and interested friendliness. Of course, you have to have all the facts, as well, but a lilt in your voice will usually elicit a positive response from the client."

- If your telephone technique is very important to your business—you're in sales, for example, and always have to sound enthusiastic—smile and you will produce your most positive phone voice.
- A phone log not only helps you keep track of calls, but provides verification of calls made and backup for lost phone numbers. A quick look at the end of the week can also give you a good idea of how you've used your telephone time.
- You'll save time by using your phone to check facts and gather information. Your local library probably has a telephone reference service. They can look through their reference books for you to supply information at no cost.
- Take advantage of 800 numbers. An 800 directory, published by Landmark Publishing, Box 3287, Burlington, Vermont 05402, lists over eight hundred categories of organizations. Or you can dial 800 information (1-800-555-1212) to ask if a particular company has an 800 line. It's a cost-free way to comparison-shop across the country, to plan trips, even to reach clients and suppliers who have incoming toll-free numbers.
- Use the Yellow Pages—"Let your fingers do the walking"—to inquire about availability of merchandise or services before you step out of the house or office.

Plan your phone calls to achieve your goals.

- It's a good idea to make a list of topics you want to cover, just so you don't forget anything. Target the points you want to cover ahead of time—you can tick them off as you speak.
- Set aside a block of time—preferably the same time—each day for making calls. If you are in sales, you should probably choose the time when you are at peak energy and will sound confident. If your work is creative, you

might save peak energy time for major projects and fit in your telephoning elsewhere. If you follow a pattern, people whom you deal with regularly will also know when you are likely to call.

- If you want someone to know you've not forgotten to get back to them, but are not ready with all the information they need, call back at a time when they probably won't be in—lunchtime, for instance—and leave a message explaining the status of the situation. You have been responsive, but have avoided a long, fruitless discussion.
- In general, call at a time of day when your target is likely to be in. It's a good idea to try salespeople and executives before nine and after five, when they may be at their desks and picking up their own phones, especially if you've been shunted aside by a secretary when you call during usual business hours.
- If you want to keep a business call short, call between 4:00 and 5:00, when people are thinking about going home.
- Are you having trouble getting through to someone on the telephone? Try to get a general idea when that person is likely to be in the office, and then give an approximate time that you will call back. *Do* call then, and chances are you will find your client waiting for your call.
- Are you making a cold call? Use the name of someone you both know (who probably gave you the name) and mention that he or she suggested you call. Your target will be more likely to take the call.

Dr. Pam Neuman, managing director for entertainment and leisure at Marsh & McLennan, the world's largest insurance brokerage firm, has some advice for business calls:

- Try never to make a "cold" call without sending a letter first. It's more courteous and makes your conversation easier.
- Plan your call in advance. Think of it as a verbal meeting.
- Start your conversation by stating where you want your discussion to go. The other person then understands the issues and can estimate how long the call will take.
- Write out your key points.
- Always start with your title, especially if you're a woman. It's important that they know where to place you.
- If the person becomes a client, make friends with the secretary. You want him or her on your team.
- When making an important call that you should document with a file memo, hold a dictaphone in one hand and pick up as much of the conversation as you can. When you have finished your talk, immediately dictate the key points covered so you have a record of the discussion. If appropriate, follow up the phone meeting with a note.

Dr. Neuman continues with some general telephoning advice:

- Observe other people's time management skills in their use of the telephone. See how you can learn from them, and then practice, practice, practice. It's fine to borrow ideas.
- If a call from overseas comes through while you're talking on a domestic line, take the foreign call if you possibly can. It makes good sense economically.
- If you don't have to use the phone, don't—send a letter or a telex. For some reason, people think that they must answer a telex ASAP.

- If you do a lot of your work on the phone, make sure that you have enough lines at home so that clients can get through to you.

Dr. Neuman concludes:

- Children can and should, from age five up, know how to take messages.
- If small children become jealous and anxious while you're on the phone, they will be more patient if you can get the message across that although the call is very important, they are important, too, and can share in your time when you have completed your call.
- If you have a long list of calls to make, prioritize. Make the most important calls first in case something vital interrupts.
- If you have a difficult call to make—treat it as a priority. Once you have thought through what you want to say, *make the call*. Avoid mulling it over. It will only increase your nervousness.
- If you need to accomplish considerable work over the phone, set up a telephone appointment and give it the same attention you would an in-person meeting. Prepare an agenda and stick to it.
- If you have a secretary or an assistant, give them a list of people you will *always* accept calls from, as well as a daily list of important calls you're expecting.
- Many people accept calls unless involved in a "do not disturb" project, since it often will waste more time trying to return the call. Others find that it's more efficient to *return* calls. That way you can deal with them in your own time—rather than as an interruption—and plan what you want to say. If you are going to return the call, try to give the caller an idea of *when* you'll call back.

Marilyn Machlowitz, who is president of her own management consulting firm, told *Parade* magazine that many of her clients ignore one of the most important timesavers: careful listening. "People think it's a great trick to write checks while talking on the phone," she says, "but often they miss the important communication while mumbling mm-hmm, mm-hmm. Suddenly they have to say, 'Run that by me again.' Time put into careful listening pays off. You don't have to call back for directions."

- If you must leave the phone to gather information, let the other person know approximately how long it will take so they can choose to call back or have you call them back rather than waiting. Do not put the other person on hold without first telling them.
- Try to eliminate ambient noise in your office while you're on the phone, especially if you're talking to someone overseas. Turn off your printer, close your window if it is open, close your door.
- Don't leave an unattended phone off the hook—use the hold button. You'd be amazed at what the caller might hear inadvertently.
- Standard telephone etiquette if you're disconnected: he who placed the call should place the call again. But don't get hung up on etiquette waiting for the other person to call. After a few minutes, call him.
- Sometimes ending a call can be difficult. You don't want to appear rude. If you know the person well, no need to make an excuse—simply say you've got to hang up. If you don't know the person well, offer a reasonable excuse, like "I just noticed I'm late for a meeting. Why

don't I call you later in the week?" or "You must be very busy. I'll let you go." If your time is very limited, establish a time frame at the beginning of the conversation.

- Occasionally, you will come across someone who *never* stops talking. Try to communicate in writing and skip phone calls.

Because you cannot see the other person (at least not yet—videophones may be the next big advance in office technology), you have to pay close attention not only to what you say, but also how you say it.

- Even if the call does not demand your full attention, do not do other things. The other person can usually hear the rustle of papers and will certainly realize that he does not have your full attention. Don't eat, drink, chew gum, or type unless you've warned the other party that you're making notes on your computer.
- Speak slowly and clearly on the telephone, especially if you have an accent. Sometimes people with accents as varied as those of a New Yorker and Georgian can barely understand each other. Slow down and make sure the other person understands.

Everyone likes a good listener. This is a very important aspect of manners in general and telephone manners in particular.

- Don't interrupt. Most people like to talk, and they will think you're just swell if you let them do it.
- Pay close attention. If someone has a personal problem, it's just polite to let them talk about it. If it's a business matter, you might learn something useful.
- Ask questions to show that you've been listening.

- Take notes if necessary. If you're being given complicated information over the phone, jot down the important points. Don't be hesitant to ask the other person to repeat something if you missed it.
- Repeat important ideas in your own words to make sure that you have both understood one another.

Everyone in your department should, of course, know how to take a message, which should include, if relevant:

- Name of caller, correctly spelled. (If an unusual name, an additional phonetic spelling will help.)
- Phone number, with area code.
- Date and time of call (and time zone, if long-distance).
- Reason for call.
- If return call is requested, or if caller will call again.
- If there are any special problems or complaints that you should be aware of before you call back.

With good telephone techniques, the phone can become a time saver rather than a time waster for you.

CHAPTER FIVE

Time Out of the Office

Your time away from the office—for business or personal reasons—should be as productive and planned as your time at your work.

LUNCHTIME

Presumably, you have been taking a lunch break ever since you started working, and by now you know all about the possibilities available to you. You can eat healthy, eat junk, or not eat at all; you can have business lunches, lunches with friends, or lunches alone; you can run errands, exercise, or meditate.

There is no "better" or "worse" way to spend a lunch break. But don't fritter away this valuable time. It's a large block—probably three to eight hours a week. Try to do something that will have a beneficial payoff—whether in work accomplished or relationships cemented or health improved.

- What about the "lunch" in "lunch hour"? A healthy lunch (salad, soup, whole-grain bread) cannot be had every day. A certain percentage of lunches will be in fast-food restaurants, pizza parlors, or at excessive business lunches. But *try* to have a truly healthy lunch as often as possible.
- Eat *something* for lunch, no matter what else you have planned. It can be an apple and a piece of cheese, a protein shake or food supplement. You need something to keep your energy and spirits up.
- Sensible eating and weight control are so much in vogue these days that you can usually find acceptable alternatives to junk food, whether in a take-out salad bar or the company cafeteria. Fruit juice and tuna salad, cheese and a mixed green salad, cottage cheese and fruit, are excellent alternatives to cheeseburgers or corned beef on rye.
- Take something from home in a plastic container—left-over chicken; carrot, celery, and cucumber sticks; melon and other fresh fruit; hard-boiled eggs. It can be the most economical and nutritious way to lunch.
- Learn what combination of foods is right for you—and how little you can get away with without experiencing a late-afternoon drop in productivity. If you need an afternoon pickup, avoid a cup of coffee or a candy bar. If you crave something sweet, turn to a graham cracker or ginger snap and an orange. So what if it's the same snack your four-year-old is having in nursery school? It's good for you!
- Your lunch break requires a combination of planning and flexibility. In order to best use the time, plan for personal or work-related tasks; but be flexible if an unexpected problem comes up at the office or if you feel that you must do something for *yourself* instead of proof-reading your letters.

Learn your own metabolism—don't follow fads.

A copywriter at an advertising agency usually brought lunch from home—tomato juice and a sandwich on whole-wheat bread. Then she discovered yogurt. It tasted good, it was inexpensive, the company cafeteria sold it in many flavors, and it came in a handy cardboard container. All she needed was a spoon and she could forget about making those sandwiches. So it was yogurt every day at lunch. Until she started to get light-headed in the afternoons, and was faint with hunger by the time she got home at night. Yogurt was not the answer for her, and she had the good sense to return to the juice-sandwich regimen.

- You may choose to work through lunch: this is your busy season; it's quiet in the office and a good time to try to call clients in other time zones; you want to leave a little early as your son has a softball game that you'd like to watch. Just don't forget to eat something!

If you're not especially busy, a quiet lunch alone in your office may be just the time to catch up on your personal business chores that never seem to get done at home:

- Your checkbook
- Insurance forms
- Your child's school applications
- Your taxes
- Business matters for an elderly parent or grandparent
- Christmas cards
- Party planning for yourself, spouse, or your child
- A letter to your college roommate who has just written to you from her sabbatical year in Japan

- Are you one of those people who thrive on exercise? Do you feel energized and think more efficiently? Spend lunch hours in exercise class, playing squash, or going for brisk walks along the boardwalk. Make a standing appointment with a friend to play tennis once a week. Even if one of you has to cancel, you'll be able to make it some of the time. If you can't get out, then do some of your less strenuous exercises in your office, behind closed doors. It will clear the cobwebs.
- Volunteer. Address envelopes, make phone calls, or write letters for a charity. If there's a local hospital or thrift shop, they might be glad to have an hour's help. Serve lunch in a soup kitchen or a day nursery. Helping others adds to that balance that you're trying to achieve in your life.
- Don't forget politics. You can stuff a lot of envelopes in an hour if your candidate's office is nearby.
- If you're a working mother, with family at home, you probably don't get much chance to see old friends. Keep up as much as you can by meeting them for an occasional lunch. It sometimes helps you keep a hectic life in perspective by spending time with people who are fond of you and "knew you when."
- Do we even have to mention the ever-present errands and appointments that dot each of our lives? This could be anything from picking up a half-dozen pairs of socks for your teenager to a dentist appointment. Do these chores when others are not trying to do the same thing in the same place. Avoid department stores between twelve and two; if you've been at your job for a while, you probably won't have any trouble taking the occasional "lunch hour" at ten in the morning. It will save a lot of time ultimately.
- Need to refresh your mind and spirit? Change your perspective—a walk in the park, a visit to a nearby

museum, window-shopping without the pressure to *find* something.

> We like the thinking of a free-lance writer who said, "I try to let my mind slow down and stop when I have no lunch appointments scheduled. If I can just rest and meditate quietly for a few minutes, I'm full of energy for the rest of the day."

BUSINESS MEALS

Business meals, be they breakfast, lunch, or dinner, are not most people's preferred time to conduct business. They're too frequent, too time-consuming, expensive, fattening, too alcoholic or just boring—aside from being a less than ideal place to work. If you feel this way, but *must* conduct mealtime business with office co-workers, industry colleagues, or clients, do it efficiently, with grace but little wasted time.

Focus on the positive aspects of business meals. You may have colleagues or clients whom you would like to know better. A comfortable restaurant—or your home or theirs—can be a good place to relax and talk on a level that you would never approach in an office setting. With greater intimacy and some knowledge of what a person's reactions are outside of business, you may find that future dealings go more smoothly. Meals can be an ideal time for encouraging others to put aside professional veneers for the moment.

In general, the best approach to a successful business meal is: "If you *have* to do it, do it right."

Breakfast

Many prefer breakfast for a business meeting. Why?

- By the time you get to the restaurant or to the hotel (most likely at an early hour), you'll be wide awake. Energy will probably be high and the mood cheerful. Mornings are optimistic times of day when many things seem possible.
- Most people like breakfast fare, and good hotels and restaurants have fairly standard menus. If you're the host, you can choose a spot for convenience' sake and be pretty certain that your guests will find something palatable on the menu.
- There's no drinking at breakfast. Everyone can keep his or her mind on business. No one needs to unwind.
- Anything that is discussed at breakfast can be tended to during that day. You can get quick action on a proposal or a fast answer to a question.

Lunch

Lunch is the most commonly arranged business meal. Most people prefer lunches to dinners in order to leave their evenings free for their families.

There are some businesses in which lunching is a way of life—politics or publishing, for instance. In these fields, your calendar will fill up quickly with luncheon appointments with clients or authors. These really are necessary meetings—and they're part of your job. Fortunately, the days of the three-martini, all-afternoon lunch are over. With good planning and attention to detail, you can get your business transacted in a pleasant and efficient way.

- Just because you're enjoying lunch at a restaurant doesn't mean that you have to eat more than you want to. Think of Jacqueline Onassis, who is rumored to lunch on just a few spears of asparagus at New York City's La Côte Basque . . . with perhaps a cup of tea to wash it down!
- Do not drink. It's not necessary for a woman to swig a couple of bourbons just to show that you're one of the boys and can do a man's job. Even if your drink is a white-wine spritzer, save it for after hours. Try the following alternatives: club soda with lime, mineral water and grenadine, or orange juice and seltzer.
- If you are the invitee, you have no planning responsibilities. But if you're the host, *you* must plan the pace of the business lunch. Actually make out a timetable (never in evidence, of course) if you are inexperienced in the techniques of combining a social occasion with business.
- Keep your main point firmly in mind: that you have a job to do. Either you're conducting an interview, or meeting with a client, or discussing policy with a colleague from the office. You want to come away from these meetings with your goal achieved.
- Don't be all business. Business lunches are also social occasions; too much "hard sell" defeats your purpose.
- Plan beforehand when the best time to bring up the subject to be discussed would be. If it's a small point, then coffee will do. But keep your guest's schedule in mind. If you know that person has a three o'clock plane back to Cleveland, better bring up your topic early on. After you've had a few such meetings, you'll see how easy it is to introduce the subject into the conversation— after all, your guest is expecting it.
- Keep the lunch on a businesslike basis. Chatter about your son's experiences at summer camp is usually not appropriate conversation. Until you know this person a

lot better, stay away from personal topics. Avoid the uncomfortable experience of learning the details of someone's divorce when all you really wanted out of the lunch was information about the metal finishing industry.

- If you're not used to being the host, be sure that you understand the ramifications of restaurant dining— making and canceling reservations, coat checks, ordering from or off the menu. Your best bet would be to choose a place that is nearby, one that knows you and where you have lunched before.

- If you plan on paying with a credit card, be sure the restaurant that you've chosen accepts one that you have. Call first to avoid embarrassment.

- If you're a woman entertaining a man or a group, simply indicate to the waiter at the beginning of the meal that you will be picking up the check. As host, you will place your order last, be served last, and probably get the most deference from the waiter.

- You may choose to take your guest to your company's executive dining room, if there is one. If there is a good chef and ambience, it can be an impressive way to entertain. If it is too stiff and formal—and if you can't linger past two o'clock—a restaurant may be a better choice. Corporate serving staff usually have tight schedules and are not motivated by the thought of a tip for working past the end of the lunch service.

Dinner

Although a dinner meeting could be a slice of pizza with a friendly client when you've been working late at his office or yours, it's more usual that it's a big deal—much more complicated than lunch—one of the reasons why so many people try to avoid it.

Dinner is the meal at which the least actual business is done. Employees are unenthusiastic about business dinners because it cuts too much into their private lives. Some married workers complain that not only do they have their own business dinners to attend, but also those of their spouses. Most only attend business dinners when it is absolutely necessary—a command performance.

If you are the host, the guidelines set down for lunch are relevant, but the evening hours might cause additional problems: If the dinner is on a week night, none of you wants to get home at midnight only to face an early morning the next day. For commuters, the problem of late evenings is even more crucial, as trains and buses follow less frequent schedules late at night.

- Plan dinner for a slightly earlier hour than most business people are used to. The occasion won't have a late-night ambience, and you might be able to end the evening comparatively early.
- Occasionally, you'll find that a client who seemed perfectly sober and sensible during the day turns into a party animal at night. If it's important to you that this person is happy, then go along with the evening as long as you can. It may turn out that you *like* piano bars at four in the morning.
- Unless this is a true celebration, don't drink. As long as business must be discussed, keep a clear head. You have a business object or else you would be home with your family or alone with your spouse. Attempt to get your business agenda discussed before the group becomes too relaxed and attention wanders.
- Be prepared for those who see an invitation to dinner as an opportunity to forget about your business relation-

ship and try to establish a personal relationship that you don't want at all. These are people whom you will see only in your office from now on.

TRAVELING FOR BUSINESS

A good test of your managerial skills is how well you plan a business trip.

- Planning is key. Your work must be up to date and your staff and supervisors briefed, just as they are when you're on vacation.
- You may prefer to make your own travel arrangements, but usually it's a great timesaver to have a secretary or your company's travel office or travel agency help out.
- Transportation to and from the airport must be totally reliable. If you don't have a car, use a *dependable* taxi or car service to see that you get to the airport on time. If you drive yourself to the airport, be sure you know the long-term parking arrangements in advance. A driver service can drive you in *your* car to and from the airport and return your car to its own garage in the interim.

- Warning: If you can drive but not too well, *think* before you decide to rent a car. Imagine the scenario: Your plane is four hours late, you arrive in the middle of the night at an airport that you've never visited before, are handed the keys to a car you've never driven. You can't find the ignition, much less your destination. Are you sure you don't want to take a taxi or hire a car to pick you up?

Planning for a business trip is also vital at home. If you have children, you must coordinate your business trips with your spouse's, and be sure that you have child care lined up as well as a backup system in case someone gets sick. A backup system means that you have thought through a worst-case scenario, and found potential solutions in the event your live-in nanny gets the flu and you're still out of town. These solutions might be:

- Your spouse, who might have the sort of flexible job that would enable him to take off a few days to take care of the kids.
- A parent or an in-law, who could step in at a moment's notice and whom the kids *like*.
- A welcoming home, like your sister's, to which the children could go for a few days until your return.
- At last resort, have the name ready of an agency who could furnish someone on short notice. It's a little anxiety-producing to leave your children with someone whom you have not met, but your husband or whoever else has been left in charge will have to use his or her best judgment.

Organize your packing down to the last emery board. This is not a vacation. You may not have time to stop at a pharmacy or department store before an important meeting.

- If you travel frequently, keep a suitcase already packed with basics—duplicate cosmetics, accessories, lingerie, sewing kit—everything except clothes.
- Keep a checklist in the suitcase to make sure you've forgotten nothing. A typical list:

Shampoo and conditioner
Cosmetics
Prescription medicines

Nail polish and file
Shower cap
Blow dryer
Travel iron or steamer
Sewing supplies, safety pins
Comb and brush
Toothbrush, toothpaste, mouthwash, floss
Alarm clock
Glasses
Passport
Calculator

Most of these should be packed in travel containers, and don't forget to replace used-up items immediately.

- Although cosmetics companies usually don't sell very small sizes of makeup and moisturizers and perfumes— the ones that are perfect for travel—you can get them several times a year as a special promotion. Watch for your brands and stock up. Refill the tiny bottles from larger ones.
- Coordinate your clothes. If you concentrate, for example, on black and white or navy and red you can quickly pack the dresses and suits that you need.
- Pack clothes of a natural fabric with a little synthetic to avoid wrinkling. Pack between sheets of plastic that you get from the cleaner's. If you're anxious about creases, take a lightweight steamer.
- If you go to any sort of weekend corporate gathering— the kind of three-day sales conference that takes place in a resort complex—be sure to take a suitable bathrobe. Someone is going to knock on your door with the latest sales figures just as you are stepping into the shower.
- You should look as if you're going to a business meeting if you're traveling for business. Your mother's old dictum about putting on lipstick when you go out to the super-

market because you never know whom you'll meet holds true here. You never can predict who will be sitting in the seat next to yours on the plane or in the lounge. You might find a new client by striking up a conversation in business-class. Or you could meet the CEO of your corporation in the snack bar.

- Wear comfortable shoes. You may have to change planes in one of those mammoth airports where your connecting flight is about four miles away. You're carrying your luggage and you're going to have to run to make the flight.

- Take only carry-on luggage. You can't afford to find that your suitcase has gone directly to Toronto while you're on your way to Phoenix. A shoulder strap on your carry-on is very useful, as are wheels on your larger suitcase if this is an extended trip—especially if you have a tendency to pack several pairs of shoes.

- If you fly a lot, use your frequent-flier credits to upgrade to first-class on long trips. Economy-class has become quite cramped and uncomfortable. In the relative comfort of first-class, you might be able to get some work done.

- Many flights now offer telephone service, so call ahead if there's been a change in plans or if you suddenly think of something important to tell your assistant. Don't forget the family. What eight-year-old wouldn't be thrilled to have a phone call from Mom on the plane!

- Because airline schedules have become only a rough approximation of actual flight times, take more work than you think you can ever do. You never know when you will find yourself in a Denver hotel room, even though you had planned to be in Los Angeles for dinner.

- If your trip is long, and you're the sort of executive who gets piles of mail every day, have the mail delivered to your hotel mid-week or to the airport on your return—either by messenger or by the driver of the car that picks you up. This is good management if you will have a long ride back to work or home.

- We think in terms of airline travel these days, but you do have other options. You could drive, or take a train. Club-car accommodations are quite comfortable, and you can work. The only problem is that there may be few trains that travel where you want to go, when you want to go.

MAKING THE TRANSITION FROM WORK TO HOME

The transition from work to home—changing gears—is rarely easy. It's tough to open the door after a demanding day at work to be faced by a husband, a teenager, a six-year-old, and a housekeeper, all pouring out their needs at once.

Although changing gears may be difficult, most women count the opportunity to be in high gear at work and relaxed at home as one of the benefits of combining family life and a career. How do they manage the transition?

Clearing the Decks

- Allow the last few minutes at the office for cleaning up loose ends, making a list for the next workday, and packing up your work for the night or the weekend.
- Be realistic about the work you take home. Don't dump every ongoing project into your briefcase. You won't get to it and will end up feeling guilty and nonproductive.

Learn what sorts of projects you *can* handle at home and take only those.

- Accept the fact that many mothers find it impossible to work at home at all due to the demands of the family. If taking work home is an exercise in futility for you, so be it. Don't burden yourself and your family unless it's a real work emergency.

- If you must work at home in the evening, wait until after the children are in bed and you and your spouse have had some time together. Then you can devote yourself to your task without feeling conflict.

- You may be able to involve your spouse or an older child in your "home" work: actresses can run through lines; businesswomen can practice presentations; even mundane tasks such as collating newsletters or stuffing envelopes can be more pleasant with help from a family member.

- Some work can leave free hands, eyes, or ears for household tasks or conversation with the family. Musicians can listen to and learn their music while they iron or mend. Artists, writers, and craftspeople can work near their children who are doing their school homework. If your evening project doesn't require too much concentration, you may be able to do it and also participate in family life.

Commuting

Most workers have to face the daily trial of overcrowded public transportation or clogged highways and crawling traffic. But if you're one of the lucky ones who have a reasonably civilized way of getting to and from work, the commute home is a time to unwind and clear your mind of the tensions of the workday.

- Read something unrelated to your work if you use public transportation. Treat yourself to a glossy magazine or two, or catch up on those books that you don't have time to read at home.
- If you're in a carpool and you're not the driver, take a short nap, update your lists, write instructions to your caregiver.
- Get your bicycle out of the garage and ride it to and from work. It's great exercise and gives you time for meditation and decompression.
- Walk. Leave your bus, subway, or carpool ten to fifteen minutes from home and finish your commute on foot.

Commuting with your spouse is ideal if the demands of your dual careers permit. You can:

- Really *talk*. It could be about a new roof, but better yet would be the sort of personal conversation you used to have before you were encumbered by other family members, delightful though they may be.
- Plan. A train ride to the city is a good place to go through brochures for a possible vacation.
- Decompress together. Then when you arrive at home, you'll be on the same wavelength and can deal together with whatever has come up in the course of the day.
- Vent frustrations. Had a bad day at the office? The commute home is the time to get rid of those workday irritations. You and your spouse can support each other.
- Hold hands. It sounds corny, but try it! It can be very comforting after a long day at the office.

Cooling Off at Home

Even if you've made the most of your commute, alone or with your spouse, you may still need time to cool off after you arrive home.

- Set aside the first ten to fifteen minutes at home for your private time. Organize your thoughts, look through the mail, before the kids are permitted to attack!
- If your children are frantic to see you, give them each a hug and just a few minutes of chat—so they can unburden themselves of the most burning issues. Then indicate gently that you want to relax for just a few minutes so that you can really concentrate on their problems.
- Change your clothes or perhaps take a shower to refresh yourself and your spirits.
- Have a cool drink—it doesn't have to be alcoholic—or a light snack like a piece of cheese if you're hungry, to restore energy.

CHAPTER SIX

Organizing Your Family Life

GETTING EVERYONE UP AND OUT

In most families, weekday mornings are *not* prime time. The goal is simply to get everyone up, dressed, fed, and out without forgetting anything or anyone in the process. Each family has its own style, but most feel they could do with less chaos and more efficiency. Here are some ideas that may work for you.

- If you know the morning will be hectic, listen to the news before you go to bed. Not much will happen overnight, and you can concentrate on the events of *your* day in the morning.
- Organize the night before. Everything should be ready before the family goes to bed: briefcases, bookbags, notes to teachers, Show-and-Tell, gym shorts, birthday presents, cookies for the kindergarten party, your to-do list, and instructions for the caregiver or housekeeper.
- Pick a spot near the door for keys, glasses, briefcases,

bookbags, umbrellas. This greatly facilitates the last-minute dash out the door.

- Lay out clothes for yourself and the children before going to bed. Even preschoolers can learn to help to pick out the next day's wardrobe—by kindergarten, they will have learned how to do this themselves. (Schools with uniforms are a boon in this respect, and are popular with both children and their parents!)
- Set the breakfast table and fill up the coffee-maker the night before. Prescramble eggs for French toast batter the night before and refrigerate for a morning time-saver. Put breakfast supplies within reach so even little children can prepare their own cold cereal.
- If your children languish in front of the closet, make a house rule: if they do not put out an outfit the night before, they have to wear whatever *you* choose in the morning.
- Turn all the clocks in the house ten minutes ahead. Even though you'll *know* they're fast, it seems to make getting out a little smoother and less hectic.
- Set the alarm clock to ring fifteen minutes before you *have* to get up, to provide the first positive psychological boost of the day. You won't start the day with that ghastly feeling that you're already late.
- If your child is a *reliable* morning person and you're not, give her an alarm watch or clock/radio and set it for *your* wake-up time. Even a confirmed morning hater will be happier to have her child's voice or embrace awaken her.
- Another pleasant alternative to the alarm is to have an early-rising husband wake you with a kiss and a cup of coffee.
- Get up earlier than you need to, if you're a morning person. You can get lots of details tended to and feel that you've accomplished a great deal before you even get to the office. Use the time for exercise, planning, medita-

tion, a solitary breakfast before the bustle of the family meal. Best of all, you'll find yourself *ahead* of schedule all day, instead of always five minutes late!

- If you exercise, use a tape, video, or TV program that airs in the early-morning hours.
- Keep a TV or radio in the bathroom or kitchen to catch up on the news while preparing for the day ahead. Buy a radio that is made to be played in the shower.
- Make your bed as soon as you step out of it—unless your spouse is still in it. That's one chore out of the way instantly.
- Wash breakfast dishes and neaten the bathroom as you go. You'll enjoy having a neat house to return to.
- Have newspapers delivered to your house to read before the family gets up or during your commute to work. Maybe your company will pick up the cost of the subscription, even if it's delivered to your home instead of the office.

Breakfast

- To streamline breakfast preparation, try timesavers such as juice, graham crackers, presliced cheese, yogurt, and raw fruit. No preparation required!
- Little preparation is needed for frozen waffles, croissants, muffins and coffee cake, cold cereal, eggs hard-boiled in advance. If something needs to be heated through, the first family member into the kitchen can turn on the oven.
- Use fruit yogurt on cold cereal as a delicious alternative to milk.
- Be imaginative in your choice of spreads for toast or muffins and keep them on hand: cream cheese, peanut butter, apple butter, low-sugar fruit spreads, honey, cot-

tage cheese, ricotta, farmer's cheese, hard and soft
cheese of all kinds. These products usually last for quite
some time in the refrigerator and each family member
can have his or her favorite.
- Use your microwave for scrambled eggs with cheese,
quiche, hot chocolate or hot vanilla.

School Lunches

- Try to prepare as much of your children's lunches the
night before as possible. Pack the nonsoggy items in
labeled bags. In the morning, assemble sandwiches that
cannot sit in their own mayonnaise all night, like tuna
salad.
- Don't put lettuce and tomatoes into sandwiches that will
be eaten hours later. Wrap them in aluminum foil. The
kids can put them on the sandwiches at lunchtime.
- For school lunch quickies use packaged cold cuts, cheese
slices, raw vegetables, raw fruit, containers of apple-
sauce, yogurt, or pudding, Granola bars and juice. Your
kids will like it as much as the fried chicken that you got
up at 5:00 A.M. to prepare.
- To keep the lunch cool, buy and *freeze* individual cardboard containers of fruit juices. Put them in the lunch-
box frozen and by lunchtime they'll be thawed out but
still cold.
- Individual bags of chips or pretzels are always welcome.
They're not very nutritious, so save them for a special
treat.
- Let the children help in preparing lunch. They will
appreciate it all the more, and be less likely to leave
it at home! Older children, of course, can be responsible for making their own lunch, within your guidelines.
- Put the lunches either near the door or hanging from

the doorknob as soon as they're ready. It's annoying to discover a school lunch sitting forlornly on the kitchen table—after the school bus has left!

Departure

It's usually Mother's job to make sure everyone is up and out, but how to do that efficiently?

- Concentrate on those who *need* to be up and out. Leave the others for the caretaker. Your spouse will have to fend for *himself* at the very least—and perhaps can help with the children or breakfast. Children of ten years or more should be able to get themselves up, fed, and out on their own.
- Get the children up at ten-minute intervals. This allows some private time and alleviates congestion in the bathrooms and in front of the refrigerator.
- Keep a clock in the bathroom and follow the house rule that each person has only ten minutes. If there is great bathroom congestion, set up a rotating schedule for the family.
- Keep everyone moving. Talk, sing, circulate from one to the other, but *don't nag*. You want to avoid tears and whining, both terrible time-wasters.
- If all else fails, use TV. If any of your kids are fond of an early-morning program, let them watch it as long as they've had breakfast and dressed before.

The school bus, if available, creates a reliable and regular alternative to you or your spouse taking little ones to school and arranging to have them picked up. Even if you aren't lucky enough to have free transportation provided by your children's school, you may find that a reliable bus service that picks children up at home and delivers them after school is worth every penny.

- Make your child responsible for not missing the school bus. Give him or her a watch with an alarm and set it at the deadline for leaving the house.
- If the children frequently miss the bus and there are no mitigating circumstances, there should be some penalty. Put them to bed a little earlier the next night so they can get up earlier in the morning. They should understand that you can't drop everything in the morning to take them to school.
- After the bus leaves with the older children, try to enjoy a few minutes with your spouse or preschoolers before you begin your workday.

GETTING HELP

In a dual-career marriage, each partner needs a wife! In the absence of that ideal solution, compromises and adaptations have to be made because every working woman with a family needs some help.

If money is not a problem, then a housekeeper or part-time household help can absorb some of the burden. But even if paid help is available, everyone in the family should pitch in. The household will run much more smoothly, and the members learn responsibility and the joys of helping others.

Children, especially, must be trained to help. Taking care of themselves and doing their share of chores soon become routine, and will pay off in the future when they join the adult world as spouses, houseguests, and roommates.

Helpful Children

Even very small children can be taught to help in a variety of ways. They can:

- Care for the family pet.
- Take out the garbage.
- Polish shoes.
- Water plants.
- Make beds.
- Wipe up spills.
- Neaten up their rooms.
- Set and clear the table.
- Answer the phone and take a message. If they're too young to write, teach them to ask the caller to call back.

- Make a chart on which you can paste colored stars. Your child can put on a star every time a task is completed. Perhaps they can earn a small reward after a perfect week.
- Praise your child. Some parents do reward children with money, toys, or other treats for doing household chores, but many find that sincere praise is the better way—and motivates just as well.

For older children, a rotation of tasks (a tried-and-true method that works in school) keeps chores from becoming boring, and can even introduce a little fun.

- Let the children compete with each other or you to see who can complete a task first.
- Race against the clock. Each child does a task. They inspect each other's work and award a point for any job with no flaw. Points can be "cashed in" for special treats.

From a Florida company called Character Builders (5673 Charleston Street, Orlando, Florida 32807), parents may purchase a Child Organizer, a packet of charts and lists that includes a Young People's Job List. The brightly colored checklist acts as a reminder for children aged five and up. Its categories:

Clean Room
- Make my bed
- Hang up my clothes
- Put away *all* personal belongings

Self Care
- Brush my teeth (A.M., P.M.) (Put away the toothpaste)
- Take my bath (Hang towel and washcloth after bathing)
- Put *all* dirty clothes in the laundry
- Lay out my school clothes

School
- Complete homework
- Did I work hard and take *pride* in my lessons today?
- REMEMBER: Lunch money, notes from my teacher, and overdue library books

Family
- Pick up *all* personal belongings around the house
- Clean up after meals and snacks (take out the trash)
- Did I treat my family with love and respect?

The chart has columns to check off each category on each day of the week—as well as a box headed "Allowance Earned."

- Play musical tasks. Sing or listen to music, and at the end of the song switch tasks.
- Have a job jar. Every day, the children take out a slip and read their job for the day. You can surprise them from time to time with a "Day off" or "Go out for a sundae," but *usually* the slip should contain a real task—an hour of weeding the vegetable garden, washing the car, helping to clean out the garage or a closet. . . . A real job makes a child feel important.
- In a big family, write daily tasks on index cards, shuffle and deal them out. When everyone participates, no one will get a hated chore very often.

Think of alternatives to nagging to help children remember their responsibilities:

- Leave notes on their desks, pillows, or mirrors.
- Stick Post-it notes to their bicycles.
- Attach lists or charts to the refrigerator or front door with everybody's chores written down.

With both spouses and older children, several divisions of labor can be used:

- Sequential—one starts and another finishes the task.
- Split—one clears and another washes the dishes, for instance.
- Rotating—one day one person does the job, the next day, another.

Helpful Spouses

Some husbands help with household tasks and child care automatically. Some do not. And yet it should be obvious to any spouse that if you two are to have any time together, household tasks must be shared. Happily, there is a trend toward more help from spouses. You can learn to divide and conquer:

- He shops and you cook.
- He does the bathrooms and you do the rest.
- He takes primary responsibility for the vacation house and you for the apartment in the city.
- He deals with the cleaning and you manage the laundry.
- You take turns making sure child care is organized. One week he oversees any problems (your caretaker is sick, for example, and a substitute has to be found), the next week it's your responsibility.
- A wonderful way for your husband to help is for him to get up with the children for Saturday and/or Sunday breakfast, especially if he isn't with them too often during the week. They can all make a special breakfast—pancakes, waffles, bacon and eggs—and you can enjoy an hour or so of just staying in bed.

Occasional Help

You may be among those parents who have the funds to hire full-time help. You're lucky. It's very comforting to know that the same competent person is with you more or less full-time to help with the housekeeping or child care. But even if economic times are tight for you, don't overlook the possibility of occasional help when it's really needed—perhaps for a holiday dinner or an evening out for just you and your spouse. There are myriad sources that you can investigate for possible reliable part-time helpers:

- Employment offices of local colleges.

- High schools—many have a referral service of baby-sitters.
- Senior citizen community centers.
- Your network of friends and acquaintances. Ask everyone you know—your butcher, your next-door neighbor, your hairdresser—if they know of good people to clean, help serve at a party, or take care of children or the elderly, depending on your needs. People are often glad to earn a few extra dollars: graduate students, women at home taking care of their own children, or senior citizens.
- Agencies. When all else fails, there are agencies whose business it is to provide reliable help of all kinds.

FAMILY TIME

When we look back at our own childhoods, it usually is not the gifts or trips that we remember most fondly, but those special family times that gave us a warm feeling of acceptance and well-being. You don't have to be a stay-at-home parent to create those important family occasions.

Making Mealtime Special

When one mother was asked, "How do you make mealtime special?," she answered, "With a two-year-old? You must be kidding!" Nonetheless, many families find that a few touches *can* make mealtimes special family events even if you've just returned from a hard day at work. Eating in the dining room, a real tablecloth, and candles make the setting festive in no time. Add a favorite dessert, and the meal will take on a party atmosphere.

Pay attention to family dynamics at the table. After all, this might be the only time during the day that the family is all together. And being together in a relaxed atmosphere helps your family life to remain pleasant and run smoothly. Family friction, while not always avoidable, is an exhausting, depressing waste of time.

- Make dinner an entirely positive experience with no criticism and minimal comments about table manners. Save coaching for weekend meals, when you've had more time together.
- Have fun. You might teach a new word at dinner each night. Let the children guess the meaning first, with points or a treat awarded to the child who comes closest. Ask them puzzles and brain-teasers.
- Take advantage of this opportunity for intelligent conversation. You might even assign a news article to an older child in order to start a family discussion. Everyone is entitled to his or her opinion, and no one family member is permitted to dominate—especially not the parents.

Try to keep mealtime serene. A quiet dinner can make the difference between a delightful family experience and an enervating ordeal.

- Have everything you need at the table before the family sits down so that no one needs to get up during the meal. Dishes can be cleared to a nearby sideboard and beverages should be already on the table in pitchers.
- Eliminate outside distractions such as television or music. The proper activity at the dinner table, besides eating, is conversation.
- Take the phone off the hook or get an answering machine that doesn't ring through. If you can't avoid a

ringing phone, family members should say that you are having dinner and that the caller should call back. Make it clear that you are not taking a message, but merely giving them a time to try again.

Weekends can provide time for family members who are not often available during the week to have special meals together.

- Make a weekend feast to please the whole family. Have theme dinners, for example. Let each family member pick the menu in turn: Mexican food, salad bar, fondue, steak and potatoes. That person will supervise the menu selection, the purchasing of food and its preparation— with the help of all family members.
- Teamwork on weekends is a great way to be together. Form teams of two or three to cook and clean up. Switch the teams every week, and don't forget to include friends and houseguests.
- Don't overlook breakfast! Weekend breakfasts can be the ideal family meal, with no one rushed and with special foods for everyone—be it bacon and eggs or blueberry muffins or goat cheese and bagels!

Some suggestions for special treats:

- Make all kinds of omelets: with cheese, leftover vegetables, bacon, onions, potatoes, herbs.
- Use leftover mashed potatoes for potato cakes. Shape them and fry them like hamburgers.
- Make unusual French toast by dipping bread in pancake batter. When cooked through, dust with powdered sugar or cinnamon and sugar.
- Introduce your family to foods that you remember from your childhood: baked grits, *huevos rancheros,* country ham and biscuits.

- Have pita bread handy for breakfast sandwiches. Stuff with ham, cheese, eggs, leftovers of all kinds (tuna salad is especially good), and warm in the oven or microwave.
- Fruit salads are terrific at breakfast. Make them the night before, or let everyone join in the peeling and slicing in the morning while the coffee perks.
- Make fabulous breakfast drinks: milk with chocolate, vanilla, cinnamon; warm cider or apple juice with allspice, cloves, and cinnamon; cold fruit juices mixed in any combination; blender drinks combining bananas and other fresh fruit.

Holidays

You should realize that one reason for occasional holiday depression is that your celebration never seems like the idealized version that you read about in children's books or see on TV, or even what you think you remember from your own childhood. Create your own traditions, customs that work in *your* family:

- Don't forget the spiritual, the social, or the historical reasons for our holidays. Read to your children about the holidays, and talk to them about the sharing, the meaning, the background, and the religious observances that are part of our celebrations.
- On holiday afternoons, go to a retirement home or hospital to spread around presents and cheer—and enjoy the holiday more yourself.
- Don't be bound by tradition. If your family isn't wild about heavy, formal meals, make a giant pot of spaghetti or feast of shrimp and oysters if that's what they like.
- If you don't like to cook, or if you simply don't have the

A department store general manager and single parent, Jane knew that she would have to work past midnight on Christmas Eve. The children were counting on Santa Claus to arrive with gifts and a tree before dawn. Her family was coming for Christmas dinner, and she was badly stressed and in need of sleep. Here's how she handled it:

- In anticipation of her busy pre-Christmas season, she had bought and wrapped all gifts before Thanksgiving.
- The weekend before Christmas, she had cooked, sliced, and frozen a turkey and gravy, creamed onions, candied sweet potatoes, and fresh bread.
- She had hired a local high school sophomore to take each child in turn to shop for small gifts for the family. The student also was given some money to buy stocking stuffers and prepare the stockings.
- The night *before* Christmas Eve she had secretly decorated the tree and sealed off the living room—with a "note from Santa's elf" on the door that said no children were allowed in the room until Christmas morning.
- She promised the children that she would get up at 6:00 A.M. to see what Santa had brought, if they would let her go back to bed at 7:00 A.M.
- At 10:00 A.M. she woke up refreshed, popped the frozen dinner sequentially into the microwave to thaw and the oven to brown—ready at noon for a festive family dinner!

time to do it right, have a festive holiday celebration at a club or restaurant.

- If you have to work on a holiday, make sure you have your own celebration. It can be the day before or the day after, but don't forget any of the usual trimmings.
- Share the responsibility. If you're busy both at home and the office, have a round-robin dinner (one family serves drinks and hors d'oeuvres, the second the main course, and a third dessert) or entertain at your house and have all your guests—whether friends or family—bring something substantial (salad, home-baked bread, vegetable casseroles, pies). You cook the turkey and supply the setting. (You might even want to think about paper plates, depending on the holiday. They don't seem right for Christmas dinner or Easter, but would be perfect for the Fourth of July barbecue.)
- Anticipate the postholiday letdown that many people experience. Plan something to look forward to in January or after Easter—a weekend away, a family evening with dinner and movie, a short vacation—and your feeling of melancholy may never materialize.

Outings

Vacations and outings are good ways for the family to be together and have an enriching experience. Many babies are ideal traveling companions. They sleep in cars and planes and they are untroubled by time zones. Toddlers are more of a problem, but once they're out of diapers, they can be taken almost anywhere that does not require adult strength and expertise. A vigorous mountain walk, for example, can be saved until they're a bit older. The more experienced children are as travelers, the more fun you *and* they will have.

- Save articles describing interesting places to go with children: museums, zoos, special events and theatrical performances. Consult the file when a free day or weekend is anticipated. One phone call will confirm that the event or activity is really scheduled, and off you go.
- Don't limit yourself to your immediate geographic area. A trip to a nearby city can make a free day or weekend special, especially if there's a children's activity included in your itinerary—a visit to an amusement park or children's museum, for example.
- Remember that an outing does not have to take all day, or be very elaborate. It can be a two-hour picnic in the park, or watching the junior high softball team play an important game.

Your children will benefit from early and frequent exposure to cultural activities. Take them to everything suitable when they're young, and when they're older, they can choose for themselves.

- Buy subscription tickets in order to plan in advance and avoid the hassle of buying for each performance separately.
- Don't overlook your local possibilities when you plan an outing: theater, movies, concerts, ballet, lectures, sporting events, benefit dinners. If your kids are exposed to enough different kinds of events, they will be able to develop their own taste and feel comfortable in most social situations.
- When you plan to go to a cultural activity that interests *you*—whether it's a foreign-language movie or an art exhibition—ask your husband and children if they would like to join you. Your enthusiasm will often whet their interest.
- Include your children's friends in some of your outings.

Your kids will enjoy it, and you will reap a bonus in that you will get to know the friends better in an easygoing atmosphere.

Planning a Vacation

- Trips and activities must be age-appropriate if they are to be fun and relaxing. Rely on a good travel agent. Some specialize in vacations with children. There are more and more resorts that have programs for the children during the day.
- For a no-surprises vacation with your family, plan long in advance. If your children are very young, call ahead to reserve a sitter at your destination. Inquire about projected weather and necessary clothing. Reconfirm rental cars.
- Is your work too demanding and erratic for you to plan in advance? You can always try a spur-of-the-moment adventure and just take off without plans or reservations. You'll probably manage quite well as long as you don't choose Yosemite during August. It's a great way to teach children flexibility and it lets you adapt the trip to your schedule and the family mood of the moment.
- Keep your plans simple. You'll be tempted to cram a lot into your precious vacation days, but aim for quality, not quantity. Don't try to pack too much into one day, especially if you have small children, and don't make trips too long. As you travel, plan for frequent rest stops.
- There are many resorts that have half-day or whole-day programs for children. You can take a family vacation, and spend lots of time together, yet enjoy hours alone with your spouse.
- Is your husband too busy to take time off? Plan your holiday as if he were going, and then hope for the best.

Even if he *does* miss the boat, he may be able to fly over and join you on the weekend.

- If you have heavy-duty careers and limited vacation time, plan *alternate* time with the children. Rent a house at the seaside for a month. For the first two weeks, plus all weekends, Mother is with the children. For the second two weeks, and all weekends, it's Dad's turn. The children get a month at the beach and a chance for some private time with each parent. Of course, the parents see each other only on weekends and don't get the benefits of a holiday together . . . another tradeoff.

Vacation Packing

Make a permanent list of things to pack for family outings and vacations so you don't have to replan each time you go away. This list will also help your spouse, children, or housekeeper do the packing if you're tied up at work until the last minute. Some often-forgotten items:

- Medicines and thermometer—hard to find in a strange place at night.
- Sunblock lotion for winter and summer vacations. A bad burn can ruin a vacation.
- Empty plastic bags to bring home opened bottles, the new seashell collection, extremely muddy clothes.
- A rubber sheet for any child who *might* need it (especially if you're a houseguest).

In addition:

- Take plenty of extra clothes if you're traveling by car. It prevents trying to find a laundromat on the road (a waste of time) or having your bathroom full of dripping T-shirts.

- Let older children pack for themselves, within your guidelines. It's good training for them and will save you time.
- Give each small child a knapsack or overnight suitcase. Let them fill it with whatever they feel they must have on the trip. Their basic wardrobe will be packed by you in another suitcase.

Traveling with Children

- If you're driving, pack the car when the children are sleeping. Get up early in the morning. Plan on eating breakfast on the road so there are no dishes to worry about and off you all go.
- Drive at night when everyone is sleeping. You and your spouse can alternate driving and napping, to gain an extra few hours of vacation.

Don't forget that your children will want some amusement other than looking out the car window or examining fellow travelers in the airport.

- Take along a travel pack with crayons, small toys such as tiny animals or trucks, paper, scissors, Scotch tape, or clay.
- Pack familiar books, a favorite stuffed animal, a child's own blanket or pillow for comfort on a long trip.
- Take along something *new* and exciting—a book that they've never seen, coloring books, a game—in case of an unexpected crisis: delay at the airport, rain on the day you planned to visit the zoo, or a sick child who needs to stay in bed for the day.
- When flying, request the seat behind the bulkhead for extra legroom. Also, inquire if you can take the child's

If you have children, sooner or later you will visit one of America's fabulous amusement parks—Disney World being the grandest example of all.

To make your trip memorable:

- Plan ahead. Send for brochures about the attractions and accommodations and go over them with the kids. Anticipating is fun, too.
- Decide what you want to see, and make sure that the attraction will be open during your visit. Each member of the family should have input.
- Get an early start each day. Lines will be shorter and temperatures a little cooler if your vacation is during the spring or fall.
- Don't overdo. After a morning of activity, go back to the hotel for lunch and a swim, with perhaps a nap for the children. You can return in the cool of the late afternoon. Disneyland, for example, has extensive off-peak hours, and is open until 1:00 A.M. if you and your spouse can find a sitter for the kids.
- The good amusement parks have efficient "lost child" systems. But each child should still wear or carry a name tag with enough information so that you can be paged.
- It will save time and money if you buy your food and drink from vendors, but sometimes a restaurant is needed for some quiet time, or perhaps diaper-changing in the restroom.

car seat on the plane; it is more comfortable and safer than the regular airline seat and seatbelt for a very small child.

- On overnight flights and car trips, take along a pair of pajamas for each child. If you have room, a blanket and pillow are also helpful. After the evening meal, put your child into pajamas and let him really *sleep*. Even if *you* know that the rest will be for only a few hours, those first few hours of sleep will refresh the child.
- On long trips on planes, cars, trains, or buses, let the children switch seats from time to time to change their outlook and their seat partner.

Some families take along snacks when they travel; others are against the practice. If you do:

- Be sure they're bite-sized and don't drip or make too many crumbs.
- Pack them in snack-sized packages for each child.
- Encourage the children to taste local foods as they travel; don't let them fill up on the usual snacks.

Vacation and Weekend Homes

While most families with weekend and vacation homes relish the chance to get away from the city and relax in the country, you may feel that it's not worth it. It often falls to the wife to pack the clothes and food, prepare a late-night meal upon arrival, do the shopping, and reverse the process only two days later. Here are some tips for making the joys outweigh the burden:

- Buy duplicates of common and inexpensive necessities such as toothbrushes, pajamas, underwear, sneakers. Leave these at your second home and don't bother to pack elaborately. This also avoids the irritation of realizing that you've left your toothbrush in the city and there's no place to get one until the local store opens the next morning.

- If there are things that you *must* take back and forth each week, keep a list of the items.

- Keep a checklist also of the things you must do before leaving one home for the other: feed the cat, turn off the hot-water heater, put garden tools away. Refine your list as time goes on. Not having to think through every little detail as you go back and forth is a great timesaver.

- Take advantage of relatively lower prices of groceries in the country. Stock up for the coming week. Carry items back on Sunday in coolers, which can double as carryalls for the Friday-evening trip.

- Use large plastic bags to carry dirty laundry back to the city if you don't have facilities in the country—or vice versa. The goal is to take the laundry to where your cleaning help is.

- If your country house is in the same state as your primary residence, you can often save a great deal of time by dealing with the bureaucracy in the country. It's usually quicker and more pleasant to have your passport or driver's license renewed in a small town. Perhaps you should even consider having your teeth cleaned by a local dentist. You can do a lot on a long weekend if you plan carefully.

CHAPTER SEVEN

Managing at Home

FOOD

Food shopping, preparation, and cleanup are traditional duties for the mistress of the house—and fit in with roles that many women, even those with full-time careers, are having trouble updating. However, spouses, household help, children, and even outside services are beginning to take over some of these roles . . . thank goodness!

- *Once a week* is one answer to grocery shopping. A major shopping trip at a large supermarket takes care of all the basics, including dairy, meat, fruit, vegetables, and household products.
- Shop very early in the morning—7:00 or 8:00 A.M.—or after dinner. The aisles are empty and the employees more friendly and helpful.
- Make sure you never run out of anything. Always buy backups when time permits and your supplies are low. A good rule is to add a product to your shopping list when you *start* to use the last one in the cupboard, not when

you've used it up! The benefits of stocking extras far outweigh the cost and hassle of running out.

- If space is a limiting factor, make a "pantry" out of a little-used area such as the basement or under the computer table, or build shelves on the inside of closet doors.
- Fish, hamburger, fresh bread, and other perishables can be picked up on your way home from work or purchased by a housekeeper.
- If you can't get to the store, shopping by phone is a timesaver and may be worth the surcharge or fee.

City dwellers find special ways to manage the once-a-week shopping:

- If you have a car, or a friend with one, drive to the suburbs or stop on the way home from a country weekend to take advantage of spacious supermarkets, relatively low prices, larger-size containers, and broad selections, plus the ease of transporting everything in the car.
- Take a car or taxi one evening a week to the largest or cheapest in-town supermarkets.
- When on foot, deliveries are often worth the price— usually a flat fee regardless of the quantity. Deliveries are especially good when heavy items (sodas, detergent, or canned goods) or bulky items (paper towels, diapers) make the return trip difficult. With a bit of forward planning, these delivery items can be purchased no more than once or twice a month!
- Some items can be ordered through a food service— usually an 800 number—and will be delivered to your home.

Lists are mandatory, but are you using the most efficient method?

- Type a master list of grocery needs; make a stack of copies and keep them in the kitchen; when you need groceries, highlight or circle the items you need. Organize alphabetically or by food category.
- Do you always shop in the same store? Organize your master list according to the layout of your store, and pick up foods in order as you or your housekeeper goes up and down the aisles.
- Use a word processor to make your list. Use brand names, and specify the sizes and colors desired.

As your shopping needs and preferences change, you can easily update the list (take off diapers, put on frozen pizza). Stash one copy of your list among your souvenirs for a snapshot of one aspect of your life—you may be amazed how much it changes in five or ten years!

Rather than deciding your menus every evening and having to shop daily, why not plan ahead for your meals for the week? Here are some ideas:

- Make a regular program (hamburger on Monday, fish on Friday) and vary the preparation for interest (pizza burgers, shrimp).
- Save one or more nights a week for ordering in an exotic meal or eating out in an ethnic restaurant. Friday nights are favorites for going out with the family and trying new foods.
- Let your family help with meal planning. Assign an older child to take a survey of family food preferences. You may be surprised at what they really like, yearn for, or dislike.
- To simplify getting dinner on the table if you're working late, use prepared foods from the delicatessen—roast chickens, cold cuts, and salads. It is already prepared

and can be just as good and healthful as something you've made at home.

• Make the most of salad bars. Take the expensive items (baby corn, artichoke hearts) and slow-to-prepare items (shredded carrots, hard-boiled eggs). Add your own (inexpensive) lettuce.

Use the microwave judiciously to ensure balanced meals when you're not home or when you need greater serenity in the kitchen.

• Many food companies are developing foods and entire meals made for the microwave. The variety is astonishing, the quality is improving, and the presentation is quite appetizing. Even prepared diet meals are now made to be microwaved, and numerous cookbooks are available with microwave recipes.

• It's worth your time to learn the microwave's capabilities. They don't cook a very appetizing steak, but they will defrost anything in moments and save you endless waiting for slow-cooking items such as baked potatoes.

Obviously, simple meals best suit your busy schedule. Yet you don't want your family to subsist solely on frozen foods or take-out. Make use of some of the thousands of cookbooks on the market if you are not an inventive cook. There are many ways to prepare food easily and yet still serve a menu that you and your family will enjoy.

• Most older children and adults these days are health and weight conscious. They will be happiest with simple fare: broiled chicken, fish, or meat; steamed vegetables; pasta; yogurt, fruit, and cheese for desserts and snacks.

• If you're never sure when your family will actually

Weekends or days off can be used for large-scale cooking. A well-organized person can prepare several meals simultaneously for freezing: for example, a roast, stew, meatballs, pasta sauce, quiche, vegetables and a cake.

- Preheat the oven while unwrapping the roast.
- Put roast in the oven and begin browning the stew meat, at the same time washing and peeling stew vegetables.
- Start the meat stewing while cutting up vegetables; no need for them to go in all at once.
- Mix up quiche ingredients, pour into frozen pie crusts, and put into the oven with the roast. The moisture and aroma of each enhances the other.
- Set the basics for pasta sauce simmering, and add bits of this and that as you cook.
- Clean and cut up vegetables for cooking and freezing.
- Take your chopped meat and stretch with breadcrumbs. Add herbs.
- Knead extra vegetable bits into your meatballs as you chop. Fry in a heavy skillet.
- Mix up a cake and slip into the hot oven as soon as the roast and quiche are done.
- While the cake's baking, cook vegetables and prepare food labels for freezing.
- Remove the cake, turn off the stove, and take a forty-five-minute break (preferably out of the house) while everything cools.
- When you return, it won't take more than twenty minutes to cut up, pack, label, and freeze.

Total time elapsed: three hours. Total food prepared: four nutritious and delicious meals plus leftovers.

assemble for dinner, you or a housekeeper can throw together a stew and just let it simmer.

- Satisfying meals can be built around elaborate salads in the summer, composed of greens, cheeses, croutons, and vegetables. (Don't forget how many vegetables there really are: chickpeas, beets, chicory, endive, baby corn, a dozen kinds of lettuce, squashes of all sorts, peas, beans, etc.) Hearty soups in the winter can be prepared after dinner the day before and left to cook while the family engages in an evening activity.
- Crock pots are great for soups. Put in everything from the refrigerator with some beef or chicken stock and let it simmer for hours. This makes the kitchen smell great, whets everyone's appetite, and can serve as the center of several meals when supplemented with fresh bread and salad. Soups are a delightful weekend activity to share with children of all ages.
- Have your older child or husband chop up ingredients while talking or watching TV. In ten minutes, you can stir-fry Chinese style everything that is not nailed down!
- If you need small quantities of ingredients, or if you don't have the time or patience for chopping, get prepared ingredients from the salad bar in your local market or grocery store. It's far easier to buy a few sliced mushrooms than to start with a large, unwashed box.
- Buy large-size pans so that you can efficiently prepare a family meal plus plenty of planned leftovers.
- Fresh-baked goods freeze well. If you suddenly find an unexpected rainstorm upsetting your weekend plans, why not do a massive bake-off, and be set for weeks to come? You might learn to bake your own bread. Kneading dough is a great way to vent frustration!
- Make "herb cubes"—chop *fresh* herbs and freeze them in water in the ice cube tray. When frozen, put in plastic bags with labels. When you're cooking, take a parsley

cube or a *fines herbes* cube and toss it into the soup or stew.

- Mix large quantities of salad dressing in a bottle and store in the refrigerator. When you need some, add in a few chopped chives, parsley, or tarragon for a just-made freshness.
- Prepare and freeze frequently used ingredients such as chicken or beef for casseroles, beef and chicken stock, vegetables. Leave them slightly undercooked, as they will cook again in your recipe.

Freezing can be a real timesaver if a few ideas are kept in mind.

- Prepare servings for one or two to maximize flexibility; it's easier to combine several small servings than to try to chop off a small portion of a larger frozen chunk.
- Ice trays or muffin tins are great for freezing small portions.
- If you're freezing something that can be reheated in the same pan, freeze first and wrap later: freeze in the pan; wrap the frozen chunk; when you need it, unwrap, place back in the original pan (perfect fit!) and you're set.
- Entire frozen meals can be prepared and later heated in the oven or microwave for delicious homemade TV dinners! If you ever *buy* frozen dinners, save the trays for your homemade variety from now on.
- Prepare frozen food labels to save time *and food* later. Always note the serving size (child or adult; one or two servings), date prepared, and, most important, *last usable date.* Many cookbooks include a chart listing the length of time that frozen foods may be stored; it is better for *you* to look it up when you cook and freeze than to have your caregiver, spouse, or child try to decide if it's too old or not.

- Periodically clean out the freezer and discard foods that have been there too long.

New ideas for kitchen cleanup are scarce. Some find it easier to clean pots and pans as they cook—before the food sticks. Others leave them soaking overnight. Here are a few other thoughts:

- Start with a really clean kitchen and empty dishwasher.
- When you unload the dishwasher, set the table for the next meal and avoid an extra step.
- Paper and plastic plates can be acceptable in certain cases, especially in the country, for very informal large parties, or for family gatherings with young children.

HOUSEKEEPING

If your career or financial situation allows you a full-time housekeeper plus various occasional helpers (window washers, gardeners, seamstresses), skip to the section on household help—and enjoy it. For the rest of us, a few thoughts may be helpful to manage it all in a relatively clean and neat environment.

> Your first task is to evaluate *where you are* (bedlam, neat but not clean, clean but not neat . . .) and *where you want to be* (cleaner, neater, immaculate). Says a wise and experienced working mother, "In my view the best cleaning shortcut is to lower your standards."

- To avoid frustration, don't clean up till the mess is completed. You're just spinning your wheels trying to keep an area tidy during mess-in-progress.
- Do in-depth cleaning, one room at a time, even if it takes all day. An annual cleaning of each room makes subsequent neatening up far easier, so in the long run, you save time.
- To simplify bed-making, pull up the sheets and covers *before* you get out of bed. This saves a lot of time running from one side of the bed to the other to get everything lined up. It's also a way that little children can learn to make beds—even top bunks.
- Always dampen dusting things—rags or mops. Otherwise you're just rearranging the dust.
- Save old toothbrushes and nylon stockings with runs for cleaning hard-to-reach spots.
- To wash blinds, wear cotton gloves and let your fingers do the cleaning.
- Use fabric softener to eliminate static. Mix it 10-to-1 with water to spray on rugs, 1-to-1 with water to clean television and computer screens.
- Hire a good cleaning person as often as necessary and affordable for the heavy cleaning. You can hire a cleaning service for really heavy work a few times a year.
- Listen to music while you clean. It soothes the soul and makes the time pass faster.

In general, it's easier in the long run to do cleanup right away.

- Wash the bathtub ring while you are in the bath. Rinse it the minute the water is out.
- Wash pans the moment they leave the stove, before the food sticks. Let them drip dry on a rack while you continue cooking.

- Rinse dishes and put in dishwasher directly fro\
Again, you avoid dried-on food.
- Make the bed the moment you get up. Your who ___y
will get a neat start.
- Clean around the sink when you brush your teeth or
wash up, or when doing dishes.

Here are some other hints for keeping the home neat. (For additional good, practical housekeeping suggestions, see *The Woman's Day Help Book,* by Geraldine Rhoads and Edna Paradis [New York: Viking, 1988].)

- Have rooms that the mess can accumulate in and not be
noticed (basements and playrooms are great).
- Regularly give away toys and clothes; it makes you feel
good and keeps the house neat. Children and spouse
should make their own decisions about what to give
away (with encouragement from you!). Keep the environment uncluttered and simple. Give the dust catchers
to your favorite charity or school auction.

Make an investment in timesaving appliances and you will be more than repaid by the hours and energy saved:

- A microwave
- A toaster oven that the children can operate
- A washer/dryer (large capacity, preferably)
- A self-cleaning oven
- A food processor/blender/mixer combination
- A dishwasher
- A frost-free refrigerator/freezer
- A coffee-maker with a timer starter
- A strong vacuum cleaner

HOUSEHOLD HELP

One of the greatest leverage factors for the working mother is household help. And one of the most frequent reasons for working is to *pay* for the help!

If you're going to have help, it's often worth paying a premium for people who not only will do the tasks, but will think for themselves and truly take certain responsibilities from your shoulders. This is doubly true for child caregivers, where peace of mind is crucial if you are to concentrate on your work.

While training is a time-consuming and painful process, well-trained help will save time for the working mother in the long run. If you've had a good household employee who must leave your family, he or she may be the ideal person to train the replacement.

- Write down everything during the training period. Don't take anything for granted. Keep in mind the person's abilities. If the assignment is new, a *demonstration* should accompany the request.
- Once you've invested the time to train help, work hard to keep them; the hiring and training process is an enormous time drain—not to mention the emotional wear and tear on yourself and your family.

Most working mothers write notes to their help, generally the night before—but here are some other ideas that can work for you:

- Type a list of all the regular tasks. Make a stack of copies. Check off the ones you want done today.

- Prioritize your list, in case there's not time for everything.
- Make a three-day or one-week list. Let your help decide which tasks to do when.
- Use Post-it notes stuck all over the house at the location of the task.
- At the end of the day (or week), check to see that the things were done and give feedback . . . especially positive!
- Try to communicate realistically with your household help. You need to know if your requests are reasonable, and if your helper feels in control or put-upon.
- Your helper may need your support in juggling her day—a time when the children are quiet to wash kitchen floors, a time to grocery-shop when she doesn't have to take along the children, some flexibility to take care of her own needs during the day. Be as sensitive as you would like *your* boss to be!
- Get an office-style telephone message book for household help (and everyone else) to note date, time, name of caller, message, and who took the message. After it's full, keep the book for a few months to remember callers, phone numbers, and messages. You'll be amazed how often you use the information.
- If you are having a birthday party or other event with many RSVPs, type up a list of the people who may call, with first and last names, so that your help will only have to find the name and note the response. Also, if you are expecting many people to return your phone calls, leave a list of possible callers and a place to write in the message.
- If you have decided to invest in household help, enjoy it. Respect your help for what they are doing, and don't feel guilty if you've made the decision that heavy clean-

ing is more than you can manage. Take advantage of the time that's freed up to be with your spouse or child, to take care of yourself, or to get some extra sleep.

ENTERTAINING

Entertaining at home is one of the first "optional" activities to be sacrificed by many working mothers. Some women entertain only in clubs or restaurants, others skip entertaining at meals entirely and go to the theater or movies with friends. But entertaining need not be a chore if you can adapt some of these hints to your special situation.

If you're not up for a dinner party, try cocktails. Beautiful and unusual hors d'oeuvres or a buffet can create an elegant but easy evening. Even on a work night, you can get home by five and entertain at seven if you're well organized. Cocktail favorites for advance preparation are:

- Crudités with curry mustard or blue cheese dressing.
- Fresh fruit peeled and cut up. If you want something special, splash with a little Cointreau or other liqueur.
- Cold cuts from the best deli in town.
- Miniature meatballs or sausages.
- Individual quiches from your specialty food shop.
- Munchies such as nuts, banana chips, olives, cheese sticks.
- Interesting cheeses and crackers or breads.

Cocktail parties need not be oriented toward alcohol consumption. Alcohol is expensive and may expose your friends to risks when they drive home.

- Serve a very light *sangría* or vodka-and-cranberry-juice punch to provide an alternative to hard drinks.
- In winter, coffee, tea, bouillon, or hot spiced cider can warm up your guests.

Parties need not require weeks of preparation.

- Have a complete dinner catered with all the benefits of at-home entertaining. You have your choice of menus, use *your* china and silver, show off your children, and have built-in preparation and cleanup. Unfortunately the price is approximately the same as entertaining at a restaurant—prohibitive for many.
- Short of total catering, you can serve one or more prepared dishes from the supermarket or gourmet deli, and supplement with simple, foolproof recipes of your own. Every dish prepared by others makes it more feasible to juggle an evening of entertaining.
- An annual cocktail or other party can take care of all of your entertaining responsibilities for the year. You can schedule it for when you have a lull in your schedule or when you know your spouse won't be traveling. For an annual party, have the same menu every year. Record the amounts of food bought, number of people invited, and whether or not there was much left over, so that the next year you don't have to figure it all out again. If it's a formula that works, why change it?
- Try having a party or dinner with an ethnic theme: Mexican, Chinese, Indian, or southern. Let the guests know in advance so they can dress (optional) appropriately; at least they can avoid having the same food for lunch!
- If you invite very close friends, let the guests help cook.

As they arrive, supply them with sharp knives and cutting boards and let them make gazpacho, a superb mixed salad, or condiments for caviar.

- A BYOS ("Bring Your Own Salad") party is a great summer alternative. Some of the salads will be quite original and spectacular. *You* provide fresh baked bread and dessert. Set beautiful picnic tables outside. Use paper plates, lanterns,. and fresh flowers for this original summer party.
- Have a potluck supper. Guests can bring or buy whatever they want. If you're really daring, don't even give them a *hint* as to what to bring. Just stress food, not drinks, or you may end up with a cocktail party!
- On the weekend after Thanksgiving or Christmas, have a "leftover party." Everyone clears their refrigerators of Thanksgiving or Christmas leftovers and they are delighted to sample someone else's turkcy, stuffing, cranberry sauce, and pumpkin pie.
- Have a shrimp, crab, or lobster boil. Get giant pans and add herbs to the boiling water. Your guests will do their own shelling, but warn them to wear jeans. Provide garbage bags for aprons with arm and head holes cut out. Cover the floor and table with unprinted newspaper stock or plastic tablecloths. It's a mess, but wonderful fun!
- For weekend and summer entertaining, include children in your invitation. The children play while the grownups talk or cook together. After the meal, let everyone pitch in for cleanup.
- Mix up the ages of the children invited. Children of various ages get along well for a dinner party—and they're so happy to be included that they're usually on their best behavior. Best of all, no need to find babysitters.

Avoid last-minute panic before you entertain. Clean up early in the day. You can always continue to cook once the guests arrive, but you cannot excuse yourself to go make a bed or mop the floor.

- Close off rooms that aren't cleaned up.
- If you have no help, clean the day before so you won't be too exhausted to enjoy your guests.
- Plan to have everything done an hour before the guests arrive. Take the last hour (or whatever is left of it) to get yourself ready for your guests.
- Keep all party supplies in one spot—candles, salt and pepper, cream and sugar servers, after-dinner coffee service, serving plates and implements. Always have spares—napkins, flatware, glasses—just in case.
- Prepare as much as possible in advance. Cooking ahead and freezing can alleviate much of the last-minute preparation. For cooking that *must* wait until the day of the party, prepare ingredients and refrigerate in covered bowls or in measuring cups. If you are familiar with the recipe and all the ingredients are premeasured, you can throw it together in a flash.
- Make a list of things to buy and prepare with items listed in chronological order day by day.
- For a real timesaver, if you have to pay back a *lot* of invitations, have back-to-back dinners—one Friday and one Saturday. You cook twice as much of reheatable food and use leftovers. For example, on Friday you can have an elegant seafood dinner with shrimp and lobster. On Saturday morning, you use leftover cooked shrimp and lobster to make a wonderful seafood stew, which you will serve with rice. You will have plenty of crudités and salad left from the night before, as well as whatever you had for dessert. Or you could make an enormous

---

Party: Dinner for 16
Date: Saturday, May 20

Saturday, May 13	Check that tablecloths and napkins are clean and silver polished. Plan menu and seating chart. Buy nuts, banana chips, wine and liquor.
Sunday, May 14	Bake quiche, bread, cake. Freeze.
Thursday, May 18	Cleaning person polish silver, iron tablecloth, and do thorough cleaning of dining room, living room, and powder room.
Friday, May 19	Buy all food after work. Set table. Lay out serving pieces, liquor, and coffee service.
Saturday, May 20	Cook and neaten up in morning. Go out for lunch. Final preparations and reheating food at 6:00 P.M. Dress for dinner. Guests arrive at 8:00 P.M.

---

boeuf bourguinonne or cassoulet. The French would eat such a dish for a week; you could certainly manage two evenings. Your flowers will easily last two nights, and you won't have to clean up twice.

- If your budget allows you to hire one person for a few hours, it may be better to prepare the meal and have the help serve and clean up. That way you can really relax and enjoy your guests.
- If you don't have someone to serve at the table, a buffet works well even for a sit-down dinner. The buffet can be

set up in advance. The guests go from the buffet table to their seats at a beautifully set table.

Has your boss or client just invited himself over for dinner? Did your college roommate just breeze in from Atlanta? If you don't have time to shop, here are some hints for feeding last-minute guests:

- Always have canned soups on hand. Mix two if you don't have enough. Stretch a soup with water, milk, bouillon cubes, broth, or wine.
- Always have a pasta sauce in the freezer. You can serve four to forty in ten minutes. Quick-frozen entrees such as creamed chicken are also lifesavers if you have a microwave.
- Make a salad. There's nearly always *some* ingredient available: lettuce, tomatoes, fresh fruit, cold cooked vegetables, rice, pasta, nuts—with a vinaigrette dressing.
- Keep a tin of fancy cookies for just such emergencies. Or serve ice cream—alone or with fresh or canned fruit, the children's chocolate sauce, nuts. . . .
- Keep a bottle of champagne to serve with dessert. No matter how weak the menu, the guests will leave the table remembering a splendid meal!
- If you *do* have a few minutes to shop, quick and elegant foods include lamb chops, swordfish, soft shell crabs, asparagus or artichokes, deli salads, fresh pasta, strawberries or raspberries and fresh-baked desserts. Don't overlook flowers and candles if you have a few extra minutes. Your guests will feel as if they've been expected for months!
- If you can't handle cooking for last-minute guests, invite them for cocktails or dessert only; let them handle their own dinner. Or order in Chinese food, ribs, roasted chicken, or pizza. If you can get a sitter, take them out.

Who makes the ideal guest for a working mother? A guest who contributes!

- Offer to take a dish; it can be bought, not made, if you're too busy.
- Offer to help before, during, and after the meal if it's an informal dinner and the hostess has not hired help; sometimes it's your only chance to talk to the busy hostess if she's trying to do it all herself.

FINANCES

Saving time generally costs money. Career women spend money for household help, for school buses, for taxis, for accountants and other professionals, for answering machines and car telephones, for deli dinners and laundries that will deliver. The career lifestyle puts a special burden on you to keep expenses in check and to prioritize.

Even financial executives who spend weeks preparing and monitoring budgets for their work leave financial matters at home in chaos. Why not apply tried-and-true financial management techniques at home?

- The first step in preparing a family budget is to identify all revenues and mandatory expenses. Compute what's left, before any optional expenses. If it's negative, it's time for a change in either career or lifestyle. If it's zero, you've got your bare-bones budget.
- If you have money left after mandatory expenses, decide how much you want to put aside for savings.
- Finally, allocate your other expenses: vacation, housekeeper, toys, flowers, charity, whatever your priorities are.

- Write out your budget neatly and leave blank columns to note your actual expenses at year end.
- If you have an increase in income or decrease in expenses during the year, why not put the difference into savings until your next budget cycle? If it's a negative change, go back and rebudget at the lower income or higher expense level.
- Keep your budget simple the first year, and add new or more detailed categories, if needed, next time. The important thing is to start!
- Once you have a budget, stick to it. It greatly simplifies life, and therefore becomes a timesaver in the long run.

Even if you don't prepare a full-blown budget, review actual expenditures at year end. You may be amazed how you are spending your money and what that says about your priorities!

Successful monitoring depends on daily discipline to keep records:

- When you pay your credit card and other bills, note the amounts spent in each of your budget categories. At this point, you are concerned about the totals, not the individual items.
- Note cash expenses by category ("taxi" or "restaurant") in your pocket calendar. This will greatly simplify tallying by category at year end.
- Household help should keep records of how cash is spent, again by category.
- Your home or office computer can be a great timesaver for personal financial planning and monitoring. Buy the software or create your own using a data base or spreadsheet program.
- Keep bill-paying equipment in one location: checkbook, pens, envelopes, stamps, address labels, calculator. Keep

all bills in the *same* place so you don't have to search for them. Mark them paid and file or discard them right away.

- Pay all bills once or twice a month. It's more efficient to set aside a chunk of time, and easier to keep records.
- Paying bills by computer can be a great timesaver, although the initial setup (listing all of your payees, addresses, account numbers) is time-consuming. You receive a cumulative record of what was paid to each vendor, which is very helpful for year-end monitoring.
- In some cases, you may want to have a canceled check as a proof of your payment, such as taxes, medical expenses, or capital expenditures. Even if you usually pay by computer or phone, keep a checkbook for those bills for which you *need* the record.
- Keep a list of your account numbers, Social Security numbers, and other data, so you won't have to scurry about when filling out forms and paying bills.

Balancing your checkbook is an ideal chore for when you're traveling or commuting. The classic method: recompute your balance each time you write a check and balance your checkbook right away when your statement arrives. Does everyone do it? No! The variations are numerous:

- To compute your running balance, round amounts to the nearest dollar. Forget the pennies. You won't be off by much!
- When paying monthly bills (phone, laundry, credit cards) actually *pay* a rounded amount (round up). You'll have a small credit balance (under $1) and your checkbook will be easier to balance.
- Don't keep a running balance if you're not too close to the wire. Just compute balance when you want to confirm your statement.

- Be sure that checks were posted for the correct amount and that all deposits are recorded correctly. Here is where you could lose money if the bank makes an error.
- Do you have plenty of money? Some women hire a book-keeper to balance their checkbooks, pay their bills, and monitor monthly expenditures.
- Need money? Hire yourself out as a bookkeeper to balance someone else's checkbook after the children are in bed. You might be amazed how much some people will pay for this service!

It's just smart money management to try to buy necessary items for a little less.

- Is there a shopping area near you with good-quality discounted merchandise? It may be worth the trip from time to time.
- Use coupons for grocery products that you regularly buy. Let the children flip through coupon fliers and clip out those products that they recognize. Also, take advantage of manufacturers' rebates.
- Refer to *Consumer Reports* for major purchases. You can subscribe or get copies at the library. The Consumers Union's testing and analysis are helpful and unbiased.
- For major purchases, shop for the best price by phone. The Yellow Pages are a real boon to a busy mother.
- Remember, your time has value, too. Don't seek the absolute lowest price if you'll waste a lot of time getting it.
- For major expenditures, delay until the latest possible moment. If you can wait six months on a couch that costs $3,000, you will earn $75 interest on the money as it sits in your bank account. Postpone a $15,000 car for a year and save $750!

- If you don't have your own credit cards, checking account, and line of credit *in your own name*, get them! Don't be listed as Mrs. James Smith; be Ms. Mary Jones Smith. This will greatly simplify your life if sometime in the future you are alone. The time to establish yourself as a credit-worthy financial entity is not when other issues—sickness, death, divorce—are your main concerns.

- Select a bank (and banker) that is convenient to either home or work. Set up a checking account, savings or investment account, and line of credit—even if you don't feel you need them at the moment. You will be happy to have a personal contact when you need to straighten out a lost deposit, have a mortgage approved quickly, or decide between a CD and a money market fund.

- Use a bank card to get cash after banking hours, make deposits without waiting in line, and check your balances.

- Obtain balance information by phone or via your computer. Monitor daily balances and only keep enough to cover check clearings; the rest can be kept in higher-yielding accounts until needed.

- When you purchase or renovate a home, set up a separate bank account for those expenses. It helps a lot when you document costs for tax purposes.

- If you keep two or more accounts (or banks) for this or other purposes (investments versus operating expenses; personal versus business expenses), your checks for each account should be different colors!

- Get a competent accountant as soon as your financial or tax situation becomes too complex for you to understand completely. A good accountant will probably save you money in addition to saving time.

- The first year with a new accountant is the most painful, as you must communicate so much information about your financial situation. Keep an extra copy of everything you provide, in case you are not satisfied with the new accountant. Then, if you change accountants next year, you can start by giving the new one the same package! Once you've found a good accountant, stick with her. She should be knowledgeable and up to date on the latest developments in financial and estate planning as well.

- Have you ever lost your wallet? Keep a list of credit card and license numbers, or make a photocopy of the contents of your wallet every six months. Keep a copy both at home and at work.

- Keep a note in your wallet, address book, agenda, and attaché case with your name, address, phone number, and the promise of a nice reward if the items are found and returned. It can't hurt!

Do you have a long-range financial plan, insurance, a will? Everyone needs them. If you're a working mother, *your* family's need is probably even greater as they are relying on you for financial as well as emotional support.

- If your long-term affairs are not in order, or if you haven't reviewed them recently, set a deadline for yourself to update your will, straighten out your insurance, and develop a financial plan. Make the deadline for six months hence. Surely you can find enough free time within six months!

- Focus on the period between now and when your youngest child finishes graduate school. First make a basic long-range plan of living and education expenses and your projected income. Will you be able to afford to

educate your children? Are you rich enough to pay
without flinching, or poor enough to get scholarships?
Unfortunately, most working mothers are in neither category and will be shouldering heavy school expenses.
- Rely on professional advisers. Discuss your situation and
various alternatives with your banker, lawyer, accountant, and/or financial adviser. What would happen if you
died or became incapacitated? It's worth thinking about
now, while you're alive and healthy! Do you need insurance? Consult several experts, not just insurance salespeople. Consider both life insurance and disability
insurance if you have a spouse and/or children.
- Are you making the most of your savings and investments? The best solution may not be the highest yield or
fastest growth, but rather a sensible combination of risk
avoidance and cushion against inflation.
- If you anticipate that your children will one day receive
substantial money from grandparents or other sources,
consider setting up trusts for them. You can determine
at what age they receive income and principal. You can
also specify that the trusts may be used for college
tuition and expenses, European vacations, or whatever
you wish. Having a trust for a child gives friends and
relatives a vehicle into which they can put gifts or money
in their wills.

Once you've settled your long-range affairs, you can relax
and rely on periodic reviews every three to five years or
when your situation changes (new baby, marriage, divorce,
etc.).

CHAPTER EIGHT

Managing as a Parent

Parenting is an endeavor that most of us undertake with no experience and virtually no training. None of us would practice medicine or trade foreign exchange without education or experience; yet, as parents, it's on-the-job training. In past generations, women could count on friends and relatives to teach them how to parent. These days, few of us have this extended network to teach us.

Even the nonworking mother has a challenge raising children. The working mother is faced with a double challenge of raising children and juggling a career. She has far fewer role models to help out. Happily, there are more and more women in the same situation, and the "working mommy network" is improving every year.

CHILD CARE

If you have children, child care may be the single most important managerial aspect of your life as a mother. It is crucial to find affordable, dependable, intelligent caregivers, or your life may be fraught with anxiety and filled with desperate phone calls as you try to patch together a network of temporary caretakers. Your life will not run efficiently until you have solved this problem satisfactorily (see Appendix II for questions to consider when choosing child care). You need peace of mind about your children if you are going to be able to concentrate on your work. Start by making a list of all the child-care-related needs you have: someone to be at home with the baby, or to pick up older children at school, to buy birthday presents, to prepare dinner, to care for an elderly parent. You may find that one person will not solve all your problems and that several different solutions and helpers are necessary.

Your budget will determine to some degree the sort of child care you can select. At the outset, set your budget in line with your financial plan. Don't skimp on child care, but don't plan beyond your means, either.

There are various options for child care. In general, most mothers prefer child care in their own home, believing it to be the least disruptive to the child. It's certainly easiest for the mother, who does not have to arrange for pickup and delivery of the child. The advantages:

- The child is not displaced from his or her environment, and is surrounded by her own toys, bed, neighbors, and pets.
- There is no travel time for the child.
- No special arrangement has to be made when the child is sick.
- The child doesn't have to compete with other children for attention.
- With two or more children in the family, it may *not* be more expensive than other options.

Another option can involve neighbors, friends, relatives, or nearby professionals who provide child care in their own homes during the day when the child is small or after school when the child is older. This option:

- Is often less expensive than care in your own home, as the cost is shared among several parents.
- Provides a pleasant homelike setting for your child.
- Puts your child in an atmosphere where there are other children. Most children enjoy the company and make good strides in social skills.

Group day care is usually the least expensive option open to you and your children. The quality ranges from excellent to very poor, so obviously get lots of references and investigate the site itself very carefully. The advantages, if the day care center is first-rate:

- It is the least expensive option if you have only one child.
- It may be near enough to your job so that you can visit your child during your lunch break. If your corporation has such a facility, it may actually be on your corporate site. Some parents enjoy knowing that their child is nearby, and that the parent is available in case of emergency.
- Some day care centers are equipped to care for sick children. In this case, you won't have to change your child care arrangements for the day if your child has the sniffles.
- Day care centers usually provide both breakfast and lunch.
- Some centers offer their own version of flextime. You can pick up and deliver your child according to *your* work schedule.

What do you do if you must be away at night, you don't have a live-in housekeeper, and you don't have a husband who can take the responsibility?

- Check with your children's schools. There may be a teacher available who is willing to stay in your house during the time that you're gone.
- Check with friends and acquaintances to see if they know of a wonderful person whom they can recommend. That will save a lot of reference checking on your part.
- Find out which is the best agency in town for this kind of temporary help. Make sure you get several references from people who have actually used the specific sitter.
- Make arrangements to have your children stay with classmates. Of course, you will have to return the favor!
- Don't forget your relatives. You may have an in-law who would be delighted to spend some time with the grandchildren. Or your own mother or father or grandparent.

Always have a backup in case your primary caregiver gets sick or has a family emergency. These emergency caretakers might be:

- A part-time housekeeper who knows the children.
- Grandparents.
- Friends and neighbors willing to pitch in.
- A college student.
- Local teenagers whom you know well.
- Yourself or your spouse.
- A trusted baby-sitter agency.
- A day care center willing to take a child on a one-day basis. This may be your last choice, as it can be traumatic for the child.

SELECTING A CAREGIVER

Be very careful and meticulous. This is not a procedure to be rushed, as you are entrusting your children to this person's care.

> Good advice comes from former cabinet secretary Carla Hills, who points out that "a lot of women spend more time interviewing their secretaries than they do their caregivers. Your children are your most precious assets, so the person you should hire should be the best you can find."

You must decide before you interview what sort of relationship you want your family to have with the caretaker. Is she to be a member of the family? On a first-name basis? To accompany you on your holidays? To live in? Do you want an older person or perhaps a student? How do you feel about one whose first language is not English?

Find help through newspaper ads placed by *you* in the "Help Wanted" section and by the *employee* in the "Positions Sought" section of your local paper. Other sources include word of mouth, agencies, and notices posted in schools and on institutional bulletin boards—churches, volunteer organizations, or senior citizen social centers.

When you advertise for help, stress the few key requirements and skip the rest:

- Do you want an American citizen? Must a foreign applicant have a valid green card (which is now the law)?

- Is excellent English required?
- Should the applicant be prepared to live in?
- How many references do you require?

To avoid wasting your time and theirs, prescreen all candidates on the phone.

- Review the job parameters: hours, days, salary, responsibilities.
- Make sure that they meet your requirements: green card, recent references, language proficiency. Tell them that they must bring green cards (for non-Americans) and Social Security cards to the interview.
- Make sure that the person telephoning is actually the job-seeker. In some cases, an English-speaking friend or relative will call for the candidate. Insist on speaking to the candidate—you want to be certain that this person can call for help in an intelligible way in an emergency.
- Set a date and time for the interview. Give clear directions to your home and a phone number to call if they will be delayed. If the applicant can't get to the appointment on time, do you really want her to be responsible for your children?
- Create an interview form that you can fill out while you're interviewing the candidate. Include name, address, phone, references, check of green card and other documents. Leave a space for notes in which you will list a few characteristics so that you can remember this person after you've interviewed several candidates.
- Be sure you see the person's green card and Social Security card.
- If you like the candidate, get all the information about her references. Be sure you have at least two references. Three or four would be better, depending on how long the candidate has worked for each family. Ask for the

name of each reference, as well as the address, phone number, the duties performed by the applicant, dates employed and reason for leaving.

- Do not put much stock in written references. Phone conversations are much more accurate and revealing.
- Don't just check the references of the candidate. Check the references of the *references*. Get the name, address, and phone number of each reference. Check the phone book. Does a person of that name live at that address? Is the phone number the same? If it doesn't match, be sure you know why not.
- When you speak with the references, check the applicant's story carefully. Does the reference sound intelligent? Do the details jibe with the information given by the candidate? If you are uncomfortable about any details or even a lack of enthusiasm about the candidate, pass her by. You are looking for a person with two or more enthusiastic, long-term references. You must feel secure when you leave this person at home with your children.

When you interview a prospective caregiver, whether that person is to be live-in or part-time, keep a checklist of questions to ask:

- Why is she applying for the job? Is it an interim position or is she looking for a permanent job?
- What is her child-rearing philosophy? Be sure that her ideas agree in general with yours.
- Is she willing to take direction from the parents? After all, these are *your* children. You will have to guess how headstrong your potential employee seems.
- Is the caregiver healthy? Does she have back trouble or any other physical problem that might prevent lifting a child or taking care of housekeeping chores?
- What education does the candidate have?

- Has she had any nurse's training or other health care experience?
- Does she drive?
- What salary, benefits, and time off does she expect?
- Once you have hired someone who seems competent and whom the children like, check up on her until you've established an easy, trusting relationship.
- Ask a friend or relative to drop in unexpectedly during the day just to see how things are going. Ask your child's teacher and the parents of your child's friends what they've observed. Talk with your child, and be on the lookout for any signs of unhappiness.
- To keep a good caregiver or housekeeper, be considerate, communicate regularly and well, and compensate her in line with her ever-increasing importance in your family.

CARING FOR YOUR BABY

You have made it through pregnancy—the glowing mother-to-be and efficient career woman proving that all things are possible. You managed nicely through labor and delivery, thanks to careful practice and coaching. Suddenly, here is something you really don't know how to manage—the baby!

Some mothers seem to know without lessons how to take care of a new baby. Others feel incapable and uncertain for weeks or months after their first child's birth. If you're in the latter category, turn to someone with a baby slightly older than your own for reassurance and guidance. Don't ask an experienced mother whose youngest child is twenty-one; people forget the details of infant care as the years roll by. And this is a job you want to learn to do properly.

Changing family patterns have redefined the role of the

father, and in many cases resulted in a greater sharing of responsibility, nurturing, decision-making, and emotional support. Involve your husband as much as possible with the new baby. He should participate in parenting from the very first day.

- Let Dad diaper and bathe the newborn. The baby can sleep on her father's stomach or chest, while Dad reads.
- Your husband probably knows even less than you do about caring for a new baby. Share your fears and concerns, and learn to care for your new baby together. Many books on the subject are valuable aids in the early days and weeks.
- Take advantage of the closeness between the father and baby to give yourself a much needed break on evenings and weekends—especially after you've gone back to work. Establish a pattern of father-and-child private times that will last a lifetime. Let Dad stroll with the infant in her carriage while you stay home and relax. Or go out for the afternoon and let him fend for himself and the child.
- Paternity leave is offered by over one-third of major companies, but very few fathers take advantage of this benefit. However, more than half the fathers elect to take *some* time off at the birth of their child. Encourage your husband to not miss this important time.

Nursing time is a wonderful experience of sharing and bonding for most mothers. It *does* take time. But once the nursing pattern is established and you both feel comfortable, it can fit easily into your busy life.

- Read while you're nursing if the baby likes to linger. Some babies will take as much as an hour to nurse. If the baby is on a three- or four-hour schedule, you'll need to use the time well.

- Make phone calls, if your talking doesn't bother the baby, or dictate business memos and letters. The baby will let you know if it bothers her.
- Nurse on demand for as long as your schedule permits. A calm, contented baby is worth the occasional inconvenience.
- Read to the baby's siblings while you nurse. This is a wonderful time to be together and helps your other children not to resent the new addition.
- When you go back to work, don't stop nursing. Cut back to twice a day, morning and evening. Your body will regulate the flow of milk. Continuing to nurse lets you keep this special bond far longer than the usual maternity leave.
- Consider starting the baby on one bottle a day from the beginning. Your husband will be able to handle one feeding, giving you extra sleep or more time away from home. Also, you'll be glad that the baby is used to accepting a bottle if you need to give medicine in a bottle one day.
- Diapers get better and easier every year. Carry a spare diaper and baby wipes in the bottom of the baby carrier or carriage. No need for a diaper bag.
- Always carry a plastic bag in which to wrap and seal dirty diapers. This will be much appreciated by your hosts and travel companions.

Experienced mothers find tricks for dressing a baby with ease:

- Give the baby something to hold in her hand while diapering and dressing her.
- Have everything laid out close at hand before you start.
- When buying baby clothes, select partially for ease of

dressing. Convenient snaps, buttons, and zippers can save you trying to jam tiny arms, legs, and floppy heads into cute but inconvenient clothing.

- Make good use of bibs, pinafores, and overshirts. When the baby soils them, you needn't change everything.
- When the baby needs to make a special appearance for friends or relatives, protect her clothes until the last minute. It's a rare baby that can stay perfectly tidy for more than an hour.

Other tips for babies.

- Take advantage of naptime while your baby is little. Soon he'll be skipping his naps and you'll miss the peace and quiet you used to be able to count on. Aside from catching up on paperwork or housework, you may want to enjoy a delightful luxury—taking a nap yourself!
- Keep the bassinet next to your bed while the baby is tiny so that you don't have to get up for a frequent night crier. Often a gentle rocking will quiet a tiny baby.
- Keep baby bottles ready in the refrigerator. Use a microwave to heat them.
- Once you go back to work, take turns with your husband on the 2:00 A.M. feeding. He can heat the bottle in the microwave as well as you can.

There are many criteria for picking a good pediatrician for your baby—pleasant disposition, competence, straight-forwardness—but from your point of view as a working mother, he or she should also:

- Be accessible. You must choose a doctor who at the very least will make an appointment to talk with you on the phone—*that day!*

- Be on staff at a convenient hospital. In an emergency, you must be able to get there within a reasonable amount of time.
- Have office hours that are extensive enough so that you can take your child to the doctor's if you wish. Late-afternoon appointments are good, for example, as the caregiver can meet you at the office with your child and then be on her way.

ENJOYING YOUNG CHILDREN

The development of the young child is fascinating and rewarding. Take the time to enjoy your little one despite your busy schedule. This is the time to focus on your child and your career, letting "optional activities" drift for a few years. Keep an album with photos and souvenirs. It's a marvelous gift when they reach their twenty-first birthday or have their first babies!

> What is "quality time"? A family life expert describes it as "time spent with your child during which your child knows you are there, is aware that you know that he or she is there, is able to communicate and share with you, and has the sense of being the most important person in your life at that very moment."

Try to keep your spouse involved with the children. Many fathers feel discouraged since the child is so mother-centered at this age. If both parents work, your child may be less focused on the mother than if she's at home all the time.

- Be sure the father has on his calendar the dates and times of school conferences, the class play, the child's birthday party, visits to schools. Coordinate frequently and update.
- Share responsibility for when the child is sick or angry. Show the father and the child that they can solve problems together without Mommy.
- If Daddy is rarely home, make him seem more present by talking about what he would say or do in this situation. The father should do the same when you work late or travel a lot.

Don't underestimate your child's abilities. Often it is parental or sitter laziness that keeps us from teaching new skills or showering the child with praise for small successes! Encourage risk-taking; don't criticize failure. Teach children that they can master new things if they try. The laborious early teaching will set the stage for later independence. Your life will be easier and so will your children's.

Add steps gradually with plenty of time to master each. Encourage them, but don't nag. Give privileges along with new responsibilities. Your child care person should be aware of the program and activity involved.

Make your child's room and immediate environment fit his size and abilities so that he can be independent.

- Structure the room so that favorite toys and objects are attainable without help: low shelves, open boxes or plastic milk crates, low hooks for coats and clothes.
- Quilts make bed-making a cinch, even for preschoolers.
- Give the child a stepstool (four inches high) to reach the light switch or toothbrush.
- Have a wastebasket and hamper close at hand to teach the child to clean up.

Teach them how to . . .	And soon they'll . . .	And one day . . .
Eat finger food (Cheerios, banana wheels).	Use fork and spoon alone.	Use a knife and fork properly.
Hold own cup.	Pour from a very small pitcher.	Pour from a regular container.
Put arms in sleeves.	Put on own jacket.	Dress themselves.
Take off shoes.	Put on shoes.	Lace and tie shoes.
Wash tummy.	Wash face and hands.	Draw own bath, bathe and shampoo, and clean up afterward.
Find snacks on low shelves.	Prepare own snacks.	Cook own meals.
Select between two dresses.	Select among all clothes.	Select clothes at store.
Hold coin or token for Mommy.	Receive allowance for small tasks.	Earn own spending money.
Talk to Grandma on phone.	Telephone Grandma alone.	Use phone, phone book, and directory assistance.

Reading aloud is an excellent activity. It brings the family together and familiarizes your children with the pleasures of literature. Your goal, of course, is to open the world of books to your children.

- Read frequently. Be sure that your caregiver can read at an appropriate level if you're often away in the evening.
- Let the children select every *other* book; this allows them to have their favorites and keeps you from shrieking with boredom as you read one book over and over!

- Make your own tapes of books for car trips, when the child is sick, or when you are away and want to leave a bedtime story. When you tape books, let the children "read" along with the tape. Stop for turning pages, and don't read too fast. Children far prefer Mama's or Papa's voice on tape to the store-bought versions—and you can tape their favorites!

As an alternative to reading, make up stories. You may think you're not good at it, but give it a try.

- Put your children in the story. Let them, or someone very similar, be the hero or heroine.
- Put in details that they're interested in: the type of rockets, the color of the horse, or the sparkles on the ballet dress.
- If you have absolutely no original thoughts, let the children name a few elements they'd like to have included in the story. This technique, borrowed from improvisational theater groups, provides a wealth of story possibilities. Typical four-year-old choices would be a "fire engine," "chocolate ice cream," and "my teddy bear." By third grade, they'll be setting you in motion with "an intergalactic shuttle," "my gym teacher," and "a sausage pizza."
- Keep your story line simple and exciting, without subplots. You can give them the adventure and fast action that makes television attractive to young children while eliminating the violence, silliness, and commercials.
- Let them take turns in making up all or part of the story as they get older.
- If you have a steady sitter or full-time caretaker, develop a good program of activities, excluding television, that she can draw on: museums, parks, nature walks, skating, art projects. Many cities have children's guides. You

can also buy books with easy projects for kids (and sitters).

- Put together activity kits—art materials, magazines to cut up, pipe cleaners, modeling clay—for an unexpected rainy afternoon or a day home with the chicken pox. A half hour in a ten-cent store at lunch can provide three to ten different activity kits.
- Television is okay from time to time. Avoid letting children view TV "direct"; let them watch taped shows at the hour best suited to their schedules and yours.
- Turn chores into playtime—shopping, cooking, cleaning up. They can learn from you and be helpful at a very early age.
- Set aside a "special time" for *each* child, even if it's only fifteen minutes a day. They can save their worries and problems of the day for that private moment.

Encourage your children to develop good eating habits early and you'll save plenty of time and arguments when they're older. This goes for the caregiver, too; lay out your rules on eating habits clearly and insist that they be followed. Good ways to encourage satisfactory habits are:

- Always have a fruit bowl and fresh-cut raw vegetables available for snacks. Raisins, yogurt, crackers, and cheese can also be good, nonsweet, snack foods.
- Many confirmed non-vegetable-eaters will happily munch cucumber slices and carrot sticks after school if it's the only snack available.
- Have a variety of fruit juices on hand and let the children mix their favorite combinations. Save juices and light syrups from canned fruit to add to the variety. Pop them in a blender for a frothy milk shake. Add milk and/or egg for nutritional value.
- Try hard-boiled egg slices on toast, toasted cheese sand-

wiches, or a cup of hearty soup for children who really need nourishment after school. Some eat school lunches very early in the day and can't wait until dinner for an energy boost.

- Don't force children to eat, but don't let them eat desserts unless they finish at least part of the meal.
- Don't make special menus for picky eaters. Let them eat as much as they want of whatever is served to the family. It will look more delicious if they're a bit hungry. Of course, be sure to serve at least one food per meal that they will eat if they're really hungry.
- Talk about nutritional concepts: sugar gives you quick energy, but don't eat too much; some foods make you fat but not healthy; everyone needs dairy products, especially women (little girls love this!), who need plenty of calcium.

Bathtime can be a delightful extension of playtime—with the added benefit of getting clean. Let the caregiver put the kids into the bath before you get home. You can be on hand to get them out at bath's end.

- In a totally tiled bathtub or shower, let them fingerpaint with soap lather first and then wash the bathtub and themselves.
- Floating soap, plastic cups, and empty plastic shampoo bottles make terrific bath toys.
- Let siblings bathe together and wash each other's hair. At a certain age (around eight), they will naturally begin to feel modest about their bodies and will choose to stop bathing together.
- Sticking wet washcloths to the tile wall has many interesting variations. Get inexpensive, brightly colored washcloths and let them make bathtime collages.

If you're frazzled and there's a lot of chaos in the house at bathtime, you may wish to make it as quick as possible. Here are some hints:

- Make bathtime very routine, with a focus on washing, not playing. Don't have toys around the bathtub, or the temptation to play is too great.
- Set a timer that the kids can *see;* when it rings, they get out. To make it a game, they can try to get out before the timer rings.
- Give them a goal—for example, a story or game after the bath.

Most children love it when company comes, especially if they can help out. However, spare your guests from too much exposure to children unless you're sure they *really* want it. Some suggestions:

- Let the children open the door and greet the guests.
- Let them stay for fifteen minutes when the first guests arrive; then to their rooms.
- A new video can be an excellent way to keep them out of the living room; for antivideo parents, recognize that it's the exception, not the rule.
- Have a sitter who can control them so they won't interrupt the party. You're entitled to some adult time.

THE MIDDLE YEARS OF CHILDHOOD

Many parents feel that time spent with children during the middle years of childhood is even more important than the hours spent together when the children are younger. Your child needs an environment in which he or she can develop new skills and form friendships outside the family, while still enjoying the safety of the family structure.

A classic model for working mothers has been to take off time while the children are little and to go back to work when they begin school. If all is well at home, you may be ready to put your career into high gear and appreciate the absence of diapers, bottles, and tantrums at home.

In some cases, though, the opposite model works better— pursue your career at full blast while you have *babies* and pause when children reach middle childhood. You may find this a good time to slow down and change to a part-time or home-office situation. If you have a child experiencing early academic or social difficulties, you may be needed more than ever.

Children need to develop self-reliance at an early age, especially if they have working mothers who may not be there to do everything for them. Luckily, children of working mothers often have the personality traits that make their mothers successful—independence, drive, and good self-esteem.

From a grandmother in her sixties:

"Don't feel guilty about being away from home and the children while you're at work. I was home all day— every day—and our children still:

1. Squabbled;
2. Misbehaved to get attention;
3. Sulked—had tantrums;
4. . . . and they never learned how to sew, cook, or iron because I had plenty of time and did these things myself."

To teach them to go to school alone:
  Day 1—take them to the classroom.
  Day 2—to the school door.
  Day 3—across the street.
  Day 4—two blocks away.

  Gradually work your way back to home and soon
  they're doing it alone.

Help them to build self-reliance in gradual steps.

- Let growing children go places first with other adults, then with older children, then contemporaries, and finally alone.
- Increase allowances appropriately and leave the spending up to your child.
- Give children increasing responsibility about bedtime and when to get up, scheduling of homework and when to do household chores.

A caring adult should be available during homework time. Your children really may need advice and counsel as they struggle with their lessons. The last thing you want is for them to become frustrated and indifferent.

- Since you can't be available all afternoon and evening, schedule homework time to suit the child's day and yours. For example, after your child's dinner and before yours if you eat later. If you've taken work home, this is a good time to do homework together!
- Be available to answer questions and give moral support. Share this responsibility with your spouse. If both of your schedules preclude your being home at least sev-

eral nights a week, be sure that the sitter can take responsibility.

- Consider hiring a high school student to be in your home in the early evenings, to do his own homework and be available to help your child.
- Create a good homework spot for each child. They need the same things you need at the office: sufficient light, writing or typing materials, space to spread out, no distractions.
- Don't try to do the work for them—help them to learn how to study independently, using dictionaries, calling the public library with questions, outlining thoughts before writing, making a rough draft first, knowing when to ask for help and when to strike out on their own. This independence will pay off when they're really on their own.
- If they go to bed before you get home, ask them to leave the homework where you can see it. Leave them a note of encouragement or comment on a paste-on note.
- Encourage them to do the least favorite subject first. It's a good habit for life! If they haven't finished by bedtime, let them wake up early in the morning to finish, with your help if necessary.

If there is a love of books and reading in the home, the children will share it. Don't stop reading aloud as your child gets older. Many working parents feel that when all else is optional, reading is mandatory. When your children learn to read silently, you can work and still be together.

- Find at least one hour a week to read as a family. It could be during a Sunday evening in winter or a car ride for a weekend outing or shopping trip.
- Stop to answer questions and discuss the book. Be sure they understand the vocabulary. The goal is not to finish

the book as quickly as possible or to read the greatest number of books per month. Rather, make the experience as rich as possible.

- Take turns reading chapters when your child becomes proficient. This gives the listener time to relax, draw, do light chores, or just bask in the pleasure of being together.

- Give books as gifts to your children for special occasions such as Thanksgiving, losing a tooth, or a good report card. Open a charge account at your local bookstore. Get to know the salespeople in the children's department who can recommend new books or reading in your child's line of interest. You can order by phone and have the book sent home if you're on a trip or extremely rushed.

- Let children give books as birthday presents. It's an appropriate, thoughtful, and not-too-expensive gift that the child can select herself for her friends. Rather than shopping all over for the right gift, you can do one-stop shopping at a large bookstore.

The library can be a boon for the working mother. While we don't suggest using it as a day care center, you should be able to find wholesome and stimulating programs for young children and a safe and quiet environment for older children who want to do homework after school.

- From the earliest ages, let them go to the library weekly to pick their own books. The sitter can take them. Children should have their own library cards as early as the library will allow—often as soon as they can write their first names!

- Make them responsible for returning their books, and let them pay fines from their allowance; but help them out: set aside a special place for library books in the house so they won't be lost.

- Get a monthly or annual schedule of events for children from your library. It's a gold mine of activities for rainy afternoons or times when you're just too exhausted to think up an activity. You'll find story hours for the very young, reading clubs, films, and periodical rooms.

As your children begin school, their lives (and yours) will become more complicated. Ballet lessons, Cub Scouts, hockey practice, speech remediation, birthday parties, all must be scheduled—with arrangements for dropping them off and picking them up—not to mention special equipment and outfits. Keep a well-organized calendar.

- Keep your children's calendar at a spot that is readily available to children, caregivers, and your spouse. Near the phone in the kitchen is the usual place.
- Write each child's activities in a different color on your calendar. It makes it easier to make dates and schedules for each one.
- Keep old calendar pages. Periodically, scan your children's activities (child by child; color coding helps!) to be sure each one has a good mix of events and friends with whom he plays.
- Make sure that you are relatively faithful in returning invitations to play at other children's homes.
- Regular after-school activities selected by the child (with your guidance, of course) can be a boon or a problem. At best, your child can go straight from school to the activity. At worst, you'll be doubling the burden on the sitter or yourself by requiring pickups and delivery of children. Think of the logistics before you sign them up!

Your reasons for working are probably at least *partly* economic. Help your child to understand and respect your priorities by giving her a good sense of the value of money and the difficulty of obtaining it. Your child's allowance is an early step toward financial independence and respect.

- Ask other parents whose values you share what allowance they give their children. While this information will only serve as a basic guideline, you don't want your child's allowance to be *too* far out of line with her classmates. If you have rules on how to spend money each week (an offering at church, a portion to savings), don't count those amounts in the "allowance" amount.
- If you tie allowance to responsibilities, really stick to your guns; give one or two warnings, and then withhold the allowance. Some parents give supplements to the allowance for practicing the violin, watching the baby sister, etc. Others feel that this should be part of daily life and not compensated.
- Give older children optional projects to earn money in the house, such as raking leaves, polishing silver, balancing the checkbook, inputting budget data into the computer. This will give them a sense of choosing to earn money but sacrificing personal time to do so—*your* dilemma!

Buying clothing for children can be time-consuming and draining if you don't organize in advance.

- Know exactly what you want for the coming season. Make a list of what's needed. If you're matching colors, take along the item to be matched in a shopping bag. Don't rely on memory. Nothing is more time-consuming than to return and return again in the search for the perfect shell pink sweater.
- Buy on sale for next year in bigger sizes. By now you have a feeling for your child's growth rate.
- Kids have a good idea of style from a very early age and they don't want to look "funny." Pick classic styles and

colors and avoid trendiness. You can always supplement with faddy bracelets or other items if your child insists.
- Buy your child low-maintenance clothes for school and play. Save the perfect cotton-and-linen jacket for when they're older. New no-iron fabrics are great timesavers if you don't have a full-time ironer at home.
- One or two dress outfits will be enough at this age, since many birthday parties are not very formal and church clothes can be rotated.
- The layered look eliminates the need for too many jackets and coats of various weights. Supplement a winter parka and spring/fall jacket with sweaters, turtlenecks, and scarves.

Small, simple birthday parties are the most successful and easiest for the working mother to handle. Just remember that the parties are for the children—not for the parents!

- An old rule of thumb is that the number of children at the party should not exceed the birthday child's age— seven for a seven-year-old.
- A special outing or adventure with one or two friends is often better than a party. You can schedule the event around your work schedule. Some parents plan an evening event and allow the birthday guests to sleep over, even on a school night. After all, one night a year is not too much!
- Have a do-it-yourself party on a Saturday or Sunday afternoon at which the children make something—the cake, cookies, decorated cupcakes, place mats, face masks from paper bags, etc. You can plan the event and gather the materials several months in advance, and the results are well worth it. Hire teenagers to help out.
- Keep a list of all your child's friends, addresses, phone numbers, and ages, typed up and Xeroxed. For a party,

check names on one of the Xeroxes and have the baby-sitter write invitations and address envelopes.

If you don't have time to plan and execute a birthday party, "go commercial." Turn to:

- A gym or swim party at a local club or YMCA.
- A party caterer.
- A magician or puppeteer who comes to your home.
- A fast food restaurant that accepts parties.
- A museum.
- A bowling alley.
- An ice skating or roller skating rink.

No matter how busy you are, it falls to you, not the sitter, to teach your child the social graces he'll need later.

- Have your children send thank you notes for the presents they receive from the earliest ages, especially if you don't open the presents during the party.
- For very small children, let them say why they like the gift and quote their words in your note. By age four, they should be able to compose a two-line note that you write out for them. At age five or six, they sign it. At age seven and above, they write it! By the time they get married, they'll write the notes without your standing over them!

Controlling television time is a constant battle in many families. A great deal of time is wasted "discussing" what may be watched, when, by whom, and who picks the program. If you're not home, the situation can be even worse, as the sitter may have little real control over television watching. Establish rules firmly when the children are young. You'll eliminate arguments and give the caregiver firm guidelines for television viewing. *Not* watching television should be a family habit, not a punishment. Some suggestions are:

- Set a good example; don't watch television all the time yourselves.
- Make other options more attractive—read, undertake family projects, work with the computer, play games.

Be very clear about TV rules; make no exceptions. Set limits on days, hours, channels allowed. If they don't follow the rules, no more TV. For example:

- No TV on school days except the news.
- No television in the country house unless it's raining.
- Let each child pick a number of shows per week from the television guide. Tape those shows for later viewing. Fast-forward through the commercials and a thirty-minute show takes twenty minutes!
- If you live in an area that shows adult movies late at night, you might invest in the gadget that prevents viewing of that channel. Children are naturally curious.

Your child's eating patterns will be fairly firmly established by the time they reach age eight to ten. If they don't have the habits you want them to keep for life, this is the time for a change! Your caregiver should understand and support your eating rules, and should be a good role model!

- Allow snacks only in the kitchen, not in the child's room or in front of the TV.
- Provide a healthy alternative for snacks and desserts— fruit, yogurt, cheese.
- Limit sweets—once a day, once a week, only on weekends, whatever you and your spouse have decided. This

helps children to learn to say no. Don't ban sweets or
any other food totally, or it may become the desirable
"forbidden fruit."

- Periodically, let the children pick the family menu, be it
tacos and Coca-Cola, or pizza and ice cream sundaes.
They'll relish the opportunity and perhaps then won't
constantly pester you for "something really good."

Once past toddlerhood, it is time to instill manners in
your children. It is not "cute" to be shy when introduced or
to ignore table manners and courtesy. Since you aren't there
minute to minute, it's doubly important to be firm when you
are with the child.

- Always set a good example, within the family as well as
in public. Teach them that manners are not just for use
in the outside world.
- Repeat, repeat, repeat! Explain the whys—anecdotes
and explanations make them easier to remember and
more fun. Discuss courtesy and feelings; make up "what
if" situations to discuss; put on family skits showing
rude behavior and polite behavior (they love this!).
- Resist correcting them in public. Don't say, "Now, James,
thank Mrs. Jones for the lovely afternoon." A secret
signal or code word can be a better reminder.
- Do you feel that *you* never really learned certain aspects
of social behavior? Get a book on manners at the library
and read it to them (*ssshh* . . . and learn together!).

Getting to know your child's friends well when they are
young can be the best way to understand them when they are
older and more independent. A working mother must make
a special effort to be home to meet their friends after work
or on weekends.

- Get to know their friends' parents through school events. Invite their closest friends and their parents for dinner.
- Start to discuss friends and friendship at an early age. It will give you a perspective on their growing (you hope) ability to select friends for the *right* reasons and to distinguish desirable from undesirable peers.
- If your child seems to have trouble making friends in the neighborhood or at school, try a club or after-school classes where they can meet a new group of children.
- If the child has gotten off on the wrong foot at school, a summer at camp might give him or her new confidence, but be sure your child really wants to go.

GUIDING ADOLESCENTS

What are adolescents? One parent of several teens describes them as being too old to be young and too young to be old. This is a time of confusion for many young adults, but they still need the same kinds of family structure and rules as does a younger child. In addition, the family must recognize their growing maturity and their desire for independence.

As the parent of an adolescent, one of your most important functions is just to *be* there.

- "Being there" doesn't necessarily mean being a stay-at-home mother. You can be available by phone. You can be home when they return from afternoon activities or in the evenings. Family meals are another time to be together.

- Be sure that your adolescent knows that he or she can count on you as a sympathetic ear, a realistic adviser, and a loving parent. Don't try to be a best friend or "with-it" contemporary. The fact that you have a career and an independent life may make you more of a role model than the nonworking mother, so be proud of it!
- Set a good example in daily life. Live by the values you espouse. Adolescents, as well as smaller children, are very sensitive to falseness and inconsistency.
- Discuss moral issues and dilemmas. Let them know that one facet of being an adult is having the right and responsibility to take a stand on moral issues.

Knowing where to draw the line on freedom and independence is one of the greatest challenges, especially for working parents who aren't home to see firsthand the social patterns and structures of their teen's group of friends. Your child needs a clear framework within which to grow, not an open door to leave family and home behind.

Experienced parents recommend:

- Let your intuition and knowledge of your own child guide you. Your gut feeling is very relevant in setting limits. You are *not* at a great disadvantage *vis-à-vis* stay-at-home mothers; they also rarely see their adolescents!
- Give the child a chance to discuss his feelings and opinions before determining rules and limits, but don't abdicate parental authority in the guise of fairness.
- Don't be bamboozled by the line "Everyone is doing it" or "No one will like me if I don't . . ." You probably used those lines on your own parents at one time!
- Once rules and limits are agreed upon, be sure they are very clear to the child, other family members, and friends, and that they are *never* breached.
- Periodically review old rules and change them when

appropriate. If your adolescent has proven reliable and worthy of more responsibility, give it to him (in small increments). Just as the adolescent is changing rapidly, so too should your family policies.

Responsibility for schoolwork, getting there on time, and materials should no longer be your domain when your child becomes an adolescent. But you should:

- Stress the importance of a successful and broad-based experience in school—not only academic, but in friendships and outside activities. Your experience in the working world will probably give you plenty of examples of workaholics versus well-rounded and successful people.
- Help your teenager to develop a perspective on the importance of school for her future. Stress that you want her to be able to pick among the best possible choices in the future, not that you insist on her getting into a specific "best" college.
- If academics are a problem, take stock immediately and do something about it. Are there emotional reasons for the academic failure? Is another school indicated? Would tutoring help? Are your expectations realistic? Get help if necessary.

Much to the surprise of many parents, some adolescents really *enjoy* going to boarding school these days. Boarding schools generally are coed and have a luxurious array of activities and events.

- Don't reject the idea of boarding school out of hand. Ask your child and the child's current school what they think of the idea for your specific situation.
- Boarding schools vary widely in terms of the amount of

time the child can spend with his family—ranging from
every weekend and long vacations to three weekends a
year. Pick the system that fits your child's need to be
home and your ability to spend time with him.

• When the child is away for much of the academic year,
being together on vacations takes on a new meaning. Is
your job flexible enough to take time off when they're
home, in exchange for extra effort when they're gone?
If not, maybe boarding school will pull your family too
far apart.

• Pick a school that encourages values congruent with
those in your home. Ask hard questions about school
policies on alcohol, smoking, drugs, curfews. Get a perspective on the numbers of children from divorced families, the number with working mothers, etc. Will your
child fit in?

• If you feel that your child is going in the wrong direction
or that his friends are a problem, boarding school or a
new school in your area may be a way to give your child a
new horizon, better contemporaries as models, and a
fresh start. In this case, you may decide to pursue the
idea even if your child is tepid or negative about changing schools.

• Recognize that a boarding school can be a safe and
pleasant environment for adolescents, but that it is no
substitute for the parents' responsibility to deal with the
hard issues of growing up.

When your child reaches adolescence, don't give up on
encouraging all kinds of reading. It will continue to be of
paramount importance throughout college and graduate
school.

• Poor readers can benefit especially from parental
encouragement and reading aloud. One loving aunt

read the required summer reading books to her niece all through high school; the teenager would *never* have completed her reading otherwise and would have been even further behind each September. She later became an avid reader as an adult.

- For adolescents who love to read, share the experience. Recommend good books and discuss them. Read aloud from time to time.
- Read some of the books that your adolescent is reading, be they tomes for English classes or teen novels. Commuting is an ideal time for this. You'll have a better perspective on your child and her life.

In adolescence, calendars become even more important as a means of knowing where everyone is.

- Keep a family calendar, color coded, posted in a prime location.
- Be sure that everyone notes their activities. The calendar should be supplemented with a list of how to reach everyone.
- Keep a permanent list of key names, addresses, and phone numbers—of schools, after-school activities, and best friends.

Talking about drugs with children as young as elementary school age is important.

- You can take advantage of public service announcements in the media to raise a topic and reinforce the message.
- Teach the child to say no from the earliest age. Reinforce and reward good judgment in this regard.
- Create a nondependent atmosphere at home. Be aware that *your* dependence on coffee, alcohol, cigarettes, or

aspirin can create a sense of needing outside help to get through life. Are you unconsciously addicted?

- The single best predictor of whether your child will experiment with drugs is whether or not his best friend does. Know your child's friends, their parents, and their family values.

The problem of substance abuse can be especially worrisome to the working mother who feels she may be out of touch with her teen and his friends. Experts recommend:

- Educate yourself to the various types of drugs available to children and their symptoms. How many parents lament, "I never thought it was happening until it was too late!"
- Take advantage of programs at schools and helping organizations to learn together. You *all* should have correct information, not just word-of-mouth.
- Know how much money is in the house and how it is being spent.

While a huge percentage of adults have given up smoking, the number of adolescents *starting* to smoke is staggering, especially in light of the known hazards of tobacco to smokers and those around them.

- Talk about smoking from an early age. Stress that it does not automatically confer sophistication and maturity.
- Give children an incentive not to smoke. Don't be above bribery.
- If *you* smoke, stop!

Adolescents are returning increasingly to alcohol, as the dangers and risk of drugs become more apparent. Unfortunately, many teens view alcohol as a safe and nonaddictive "high." While you may prefer alcohol to other drugs, your goal should be to have them both alcohol *and* drug free.

- Stress that alcohol abuse can be very dangerous to the health of a growing and developing teen.
- Try to be sure that your teenage child is not a passenger in cars driven by others who have been drinking. Offer to pick him or her up no matter where or when, if their means of sober transportation falls through.
- Help to create alcohol-free events that will attract your children and their friends; dances, parties, sporting events. Serve good food and nonalcoholic drinks.

One of the best ways to deal with parenting of an adolescent is to create a parent network, formal or informal. You may find it easier to create a working-parent network—possibly getting together after work or in the early evening.

- Discuss your observations, feelings, and fears. You will be able to find a group of parents who espouse the same values and share the same concerns as you. There's strength in numbers!
- Dispel or confirm statements such as "All the other kids do it." You should know the facts, not a biased interpretation of them. Of course, even if all the other kids *do* "do it," it need not mean that *yours* should!
- Work together with other parents to create healthy activities and events for adolescents. A parental impetus and budget will help the children to get otherwise impossible projects off the ground.
- If you don't have a network, start one. Advertise in the school's newspaper for parents with similar concerns. Post a notice in the school. Ask the school administration for help in finding like-minded parents.

Until your children go away to school, they must endure some parental supervision. It is still your right to establish some rules.

- Be sure that there is adult supervision of all parties and social events. Supervising need not mean interfering. Stay in the background where your presence is known but not a burden.
- Have a definite start and end to social events. If you're the host, decide the time to end the party and stick to it.
- Be sure that guest lists are made and that uninvited guests don't crash. Your teen can be expected to select guests and encourage their behavior based on your family rules. Uninvited guests are often the cause of rule-breaking.
- Be sure that you know where your child is and when she'll be home. If there is a change in plans, insist that she call you, no matter what time of day or night.
- Be sure your child can reach you or another adult when she's at a party or an event. You never know when the situation will be uncomfortable and she will want to be able to turn to you to take her home or make an excuse for leaving.

At a certain age, it is the telephone, not the television, that becomes the problem. If you don't believe in (or don't want to pay for) a separate phone for the children, here are some hints:

- Set strict hours when they may talk: 8:00 to 9:00 P.M., one hour after school, never after 11:00 P.M., or whatever.
- Insist on fifteen minutes on, fifteen minutes off in case someone is trying to reach you.

- Get call-waiting so that you won't miss a call. Make it a family rule that if a call comes in for someone else, the talker must take a message and then get off within a few minutes so the call can be returned.
- Let your teenagers pay for their own long-distance phone calls.

"Living with adolescents is like living with permanent houseguests," laments one mother. If this is true in your home, make sure *yours* are the kind of houseguests who clean up their rooms!

- Teenagers (even boys) should know how to wash and fold their own clothes. After all, they'll soon be on their own.
- They should be expected to clean up their rooms completely on a regular basis, but that may not be daily.
- Withhold certain privileges for those with messy rooms—reduced allowance, no car privileges, or whatever is important to your teen.
- If repeated warnings don't work, give them twenty-four hours' notice that you'll scoop up everything out of place and lock it up for a week. The second time the item gets scooped up, you are justified in giving it away to your favorite charity!

Older children should take the responsibility for getting enough sleep to function properly at school.

- Set a time after which things must be quiet in the home—no more music, television, or radio. Let the kids do homework, read, or pursue hobbies if they aren't ready to fall asleep. You will need the peace and quiet as much as they do if your work life is to succeed.
- Make teenagers responsible for getting themselves up in

the morning. Get them an alarm clock or clock radio.

Teach your teenager good manners and he or she will be comfortable anywhere. Knowing how to behave and what to do takes away much of the tension from social events. If you've left social training to unqualified caregivers, it's never too late to remedy the situation. Here are some tips:

- Include adolescents in situations where they can observe and learn good manners—dinners, restaurants, receptions, receiving lines.
- Never criticize them publicly.
- Recap social behavior the next day, pointing out where others (not your child) behaved correctly or incorrectly.
- Of course, offer praise to your own teen, if warranted.

As your children approach adulthood, they will be in a better position to understand your work and the trade-offs you have had to make to manage it all. They are also more likely to criticize and to blame you. They will pick your most vulnerable spot, which may be your sense of guilt for working. Be prepared and let most of it roll off your back.

Do not allow youngsters to capitalize on any guilt feelings you may have because you enjoy your career. They go through periods of resentment and manipulation. Tell them what you do, and, if possible, let them see you at work. As they mature, the resentment will recede and pride will take its place.

Develop joint interests. Sports like tennis, riding, and skiing are particularly good ways to keep the family together. If you're not good at any of these activities, don't despair. You *can* learn!

- Activities like skating, shopping, museums, or movies can be ways of sharing teenagers' interests. Take your cue from them, but don't be hurt if they usually want to spend time with their peers. Just keep trying to reach out. Make a thousand suggestions and maybe a few will be accepted.

- Family vacations in ski or beach resorts are great ways to reestablish contact with adolescents. You can be independent during the day and enjoy breakfasts and dinners together in an atmosphere of health and relaxation.
- If you can't take time off because of your job, try to find ways that your child can be with you at work.
- In your office, let them earn extra money as a temp, filing, doing phone canvassing, researching, sitting in for staff on vacation.
- Let your teens observe you at work and possibly write an article for the school paper. Even just being an observer in some fields can be a good résumé builder for the future.
- Create an exchange program with children of other working mothers. The son of an attorney may enjoy a week in a physician's office, if he's already spent time at Mom's law firm. Your teenage daughter may love to help out in the creative department of an ad agency while you take your friend's child to your art gallery during spring break.

SINGLE PARENTING

Any woman with a career and family sometimes feels like a beast of burden carrying the physical and emotional baggage of the family *and* work. But if the married mother feels like a pack horse in the foothills, the single mother is the camel crossing the desert—or may feel like it when times are especially tough.

The logistics of managing it all without a spouse or equivalent person to share the work are complex. But most single mothers point to the weight of making each decision alone as the most difficult part of their lives. It is the lack of someone to shoulder the emotional burden from time to time, rather than the frenzied schedule, that is more likely to wear you out.

The best advice from those who know is:

- Set realistic goals for yourself. If you can keep the family, a career, and a household running without frequent disasters, you're doing very well.
- Learn to ask for and accept help whenever and wherever it's offered. Any responsibility, expense, or chore that you can share with someone else will give you time to marshal your forces and be better as a mother and career woman.
- The children need many sources of adult support and guidance. Open new avenues for relationships with caring and stable adults, especially if you are going through a particularly difficult period emotionally. Clubs, scouting, Big Brothers, all are sources of capable adults.

Volumes have been written on divorce and its impact on you and the children (see, for example, *The Dollars and Sense of Divorce,* by Dr. Judith Briles [New York: Master Media Limited, 1988]). Here are some thoughts aimed at the divorced working mother who is trying to manage it all:

- Don't let the divorce process take over your whole life. Let your career, studies, or children become such vibrant parts of your life that the divorce proceedings can take a backseat.

- If the children spend time with their father on weekends or evenings, this can be personal time for you to relax, date, or develop new interests and friendships.
- The child should be able to keep contact with both sets of grandparents if at all feasible. Work especially hard to keep the doors open to that generation (great-aunts and great-uncles will do) even if your relationship with the ex-spouse is closed.
- Get the children a puppy or kitten if they seem to need a source of friendship and security during a difficult time.

The severe illness or death of a parent may leave your children feeling particularly vulnerable. Their recurring fear after losing their father may be "What if something should happen to Mommy?" While most children feel that their parents, like themselves, are immortal, the child who has lost a parent feels less secure, knowing that parents are not necessarily there forever. While the extraordinary complexity of this issue is far beyond the scope of this book, there are a few thoughts that other mothers have shared that may help:

- Make an extra effort to be present in the child's life; reassure her that you are there and you are fine. Call her every afternoon after school. If she sleeps at a friend's home, call to wish her good night.
- Know your child's schedule so that you can be part of her daily life even when you are working or away. Call to wish her luck a few minutes before her baseball team leaves for the field; leave her a special surprise or note on the day she is in the school play if you can't be there. Let her know that you are with her in spirit.
- Always be sure she has a way to reach you. Leave your phone number and reassure her that her call will always be important. After all, it is!

- Try to keep the other elements of your child's life as stable as possible for as long as possible. Keeping the same home, same school, same caregivers, is important in helping your child rebuild her sense of security and confidence.

Do you feel that life seems to revolve around couples? That social events and entertaining are twice as difficult for one? Single mothers suggest:

- One benefit of being a single parent is that expectations of your entertaining in a grand style may be lowered. Take advantage of this perception to have a casual and fun party rather than a formal dinner.
- Parties need not have an equal number of men and women. Don't have a sit-down dinner; have a buffet or cocktail party where the male/female ratio is not obvious.
- Invite single women and have each bring a single man who will *not* be her date.
- Try to do interesting things in a group—the theater, the local folk festival, a book club.
- Take a couple out to dinner if they've entertained you at their home. Or to brunch!
- Have a major party every few years to pay back invitations you've received and to get your friends together. A brunch and concert make a lovely Sunday-afternoon party that you can host.
- Find ways to include the children. Suggest to other single mothers that you all take the children to an activity or event.

Single parents are carrying an extra-heavy burden. Wouldn't you think that people would realize that and stop asking you to give more? Sadly, this is not the case; happily, you have a good excuse to say no!

- Decide what you *enjoy* doing and let others know. If you like chaperoning a class trip but can't stand selling raffle tickets, volunteer to be the chaperone!
- Don't feel guilty regarding other parents, your job, or your children. Your situation, while not unique, deserves special treatment. You cannot be expected to drive the boys to Little League every Wednesday if you work full-time.
- Simplify. Don't give in to buying a rabbit just because your daughter's best friend got one. Let your children decide between a movie or the zoo on Saturday afternoon, don't try to do *both*.

> "While I was typing quite a bit for graduate school, my daughter had her own typewriter to work on in the same room as mine. She felt less compelled to distract me if we were working side by side. When I had sewing to do, she 'had sewing to do.' Typewriters, sewing kits, desks, and office supplies were as critical to my child-rearing as playhouses and dolls were to my mother's."

You will certainly have times when you don't feel up to being superwoman at home and work. Know your limits, and if you're too stressed, take a little time from both career and children to cool off. If you sometimes feel unable to cope with the immediate demands, you are not alone. Here are some suggestions from single mothers:

- If you're extremely tense, don't rush home to eat supper with the children. Go home after they're in bed. Eat alone. Give yourself time to unwind. Says one mother, "Sometimes if I'm too tense from the day's activities, it's best if I don't eat with the kids because meals can then be an unpleasant time. I try to avoid dramas during eating times."

- Explain to the children that Mama sometimes gets tired and needs a peaceful time. Settle yourself in the living room, relax, and then let them join you (one by one) to talk quietly. You'll be amazed how even little children can understand and appreciate the healing nature of quiet and calm. There are also books for children explaining why they should like five minutes of peace and quiet, too.

There *are* some positive aspects to raising a child and managing your career alone. You can reach a decision and stick to it without having to negotiate with your spouse. A negative atmosphere of fighting or coldness will not be present in your home. Your child will no longer have to compete with his father for your time. Make the most of the good parts of being single—the closeness of a happy family with time for each person.

- Be open-minded and develop the ability to be resourceful and spontaneous.
- Don't feel inadequate or lost if you're doing things other than "by the book."
- Relax. Take one thing at a time.
- Put a lot of love into everything you do. Your children will be fine.

CHAPTER NINE

Finding Time for Yourself

One mother remembers the time she packed for a trip—each child's clothes neatly organized, with matching socks and underwear for each day, toothbrushes, rainy day supplies, medicines. She was exhausted but relieved to finally shut the suitcases. When she arrived at her destination and opened the luggage, she realized the worst: she had forgotten to pack for herself.

Many working mothers have a similar situation *every day*. In their rush to get everyone else up and out, they are sometimes the forgotten ones, leaving for work without makeup, polished shoes, or combed hair.

While "beauty is in the eye of the beholder," it still plays an important role in the development of confidence among 80 percent of the women surveyed in *The Keri Report: Confidence and the American Woman,* a major survey conducted in 1988 for Westwood Pharmaceuticals. Over half the women polled regularly use facial moisturizer, and nearly six in ten use body lotion several times a week. Sixty percent exercise at

least three times a week, and two-thirds use makeup frequently. Married women tend to exercise a little less often
and spend somewhat less time using beauty products—possibly because they are busier than unmarried women, or
because they feel they already "have their man."

With all the attention we pay to managing the rest of our
lives, sometimes it seems there's no time left over to care for
ourselves. But that's shortsighted: *The Keri Report* shows a
clear relationship between a woman's level of confidence and
the amount of time she spends caring for her appearance.
We should learn to think of the time spent on ourselves as a
necessity rather than a luxury—an investment in our personal and professional success.

GROOMING AND WARDROBE

A simple, neat hairdo is key to timesaving in the morning. A
short "wash and wear" style looks professional with minimal
care.

- If your hair needs more attention, keep hot curlers next
  to the alarm clock. When it rings, plug in the rollers,
  press "snooze" on your alarm, and enjoy an extra ten
  minutes in bed while the curlers heat up.
- Use a clear plastic cookbook holder to support a magazine or book to read while you blow-dry your hair.
- If you're going out in the evening, let your child hold the
  dryer while you blow-dry your hair or do your nails. It's a
  chance to talk and be together.

Makeup can be put on in a few minutes in front of your
mirror in the morning if you are well organized. Avoid the
temptation to apply it on the fly—at stoplights, in cars or

Nelson Lee Novick, M.D., author of *Super Skin* and *Saving Face*, and clinic chief of the Department of Dermatology, Mt. Sinai Medical Center in New York City, suggests these basics for skin care on the run.

"To maintain healthy skin, the three basics of good care are a cleanser, a moisturizer, and a sunscreen.

"Cleansing skin with soap and water removes most environmental and natural skin surface substances, such as dirt, cosmetics, oils, bacteria, and sweat. For people with normal skin, a plain basic soap will do the job of cleaning efficiently. But for people with very sensitive skin, some soaps are drying and irritating. In that case, soaps which contain moisturizers or synthetic soaps, such as Lowila Cake, are recommended. However, almost any soap or detergent cleanser, no matter how good, can still be somewhat drying—a problem that can be minimized by not overscrubbing the skin.

"Americans can be overzealous about bathing, which is extremely drying to the skin. For those who don't want to give up the pleasures of a bath, it's important to use a moisturizing bath oil rather than perfumed oils, bubble baths, or powders that can be irritating. Adding two or three capfuls of a bath oil, such as Alpha Keri, to the water helps.

"The major function of moisturizers is to protect the skin from excessive dryness by preventing water loss. You don't need a special moisturizer for each different part of your body. When choosing a moisturizer, however, look for one that is noncomedogenic, meaning it will not promote acne, and one that is free of lanolin, a common skin irritant."

taxis, in the elevator or at work. The results will never be as good, and you risk going through the day with an embarrassing smudge if you haven't used a good mirror. You must spend at least a little time on your own pulled-together look!

- Select your brand of day makeup and buy two of everything—one for home, one for office. Take advantage of sales and promotions of your brand to stock up on spares. The smaller sizes offered in promotions make terrific travel makeup and allow you to try new colors. If you don't like the color in the tiny promotional bottle of foundation, wash out the bottle and substitute your own color.
- Keep your day makeup close at hand in the bathroom. Your evening makeup can be organized in a separate box for when you have more time to select colors and try a new look.
- Periodically ask a trusted friend how your makeup looks. We need feedback and rarely get it unless we ask!
- If you are inexpert in selecting colors and applying makeup, take advantage of the free advice offered at beauty counters. They will help you pick colors and show you how to apply makeup that will be flattering to you. Just be sure to set a budget of what you will spend on makeup after the "makeover" or you may find yourself with hundreds of dollars' worth of "necessities."
- Office makeup supplies should duplicate what you have at home. Keep office makeup in a small leather pouch; don't be seen walking to the ladies' room with a brightly flowered zipper bag—very tacky.

When building your wardrobe, select classic clothes appropriate to any occasion, so that few decisions have to be made each day and so that a change of plans for the evening won't require going home to change. Keep a few dressy accessories in your office to glamorize your outfit for the evening.

- Keep colors in the same color family so that you can match all with a few accessories and can interchange clothing for new looks. This simplifies packing for business trips and speeds up shopping.
- Use catalogues to shop for clothes. They have extremely liberal return policies if you make a mistake. If you have hard-to-fit feet use catalogues for shoe shopping, too. There is often a bigger selection of very narrow or wide shoes in catalogues than in shoe stores.
- Set aside a *day* for semiannual shopping; plan your needs and review this year's styles via magazines and catalogues; make a list and don't forget shoes, stockings, and other accessories.
- Dressing appropriately for the shopping trip is important. Wear something easy to slip on and off. Wear or take a blouse in case you need to try on suits, skirts, or pants. Avoid earrings and jewelry that need to be removed. If you're wearing flat shoes, take along a pair of heels for trying on dresses.
- Be well dressed for shopping, and the sales help will make an extra effort. They're delighted to find an efficient customer who wants to buy and can afford it.
- Avoid fad clothing and impulse buying. If you are an impulsive shopper, shop one day but don't buy. Note the salesperson's name, the item number and description, and the price. Then order by phone the items you really want after a lot of reflection and a good night's sleep. Pay by credit card and have the items delivered.
- Know what colors really flatter you. The year when *your* colors are in style, stock up on wardrobe staples such as classic sweaters, pocketbooks, solid color skirts, and scarves. Next year the fashion may change to purple and orange! Of course, avoid styles that will be outdated in coming years.

- Shop for clothing during vacations or in resorts. The selection is new and it won't feel like a chore.
- For the extremely busy career woman, many large department stores have executive shopping departments. Once you register your sizes and preferences, the "personal shopper" will do your work for you. You let them know what you need and they find it. There may be a fee, and they may not search out the least expensive alternatives, but if you're willing to pay the price, it can be a timesaver.

Other timesavers:

- Keep your "work" jewelry in the bathroom near your makeup so that you can put yourself together without extra steps. Keep jewelry sparkling by dipping in all-purpose household cleansers or in ammonia.
- Save money on pantyhose. When you get a run in one stocking leg, cut off that leg and save the rest. Wear it with another "half pair" of the same shade.
- If you need glasses, have enough pairs to keep one near your bed, one in the office, and one in the car.
- If you need several handbags, get a compartmentalized holder for your purse to hold money, makeup, keys, papers. A zippered makeup holder is an inexpensive solution. Then, when you change handbags, you only have to move a few items.

Your two basic wardrobes, summer and winter, must be rotated.

- Decide in advance the date when you will make the transition. Don't worry about the weather. You won't be off by more than a week or so.

- Set aside the time to switch your closet. Really put the off-season clothes *away*—in the attic or a far closet. If you only have one closet, use the far end and don't rifle through the clothes once they're "away."
- To manage the seasonal transition, choose layered clothing so you don't have to worry about the weather.
- Your closet and drawers should contain only clean, mended, ironed clothing—ready to wear. Check hems, buttons, snaps, for spots and wrinkles *before* putting clothes away.
- Listen to the weather forecast Sunday night and plan your outfits for the entire workweek. You'll know if something needs to be cleaned; you'll have the right stockings. And you won't need to replan until the weekend!
- Decide what to wear before going to bed. For those who must see the dawn to decide, narrow your choices to two or three outfits and center them in the closet for the morning.
- If your schedule is hectic, save clothes care for the weekend or other block of time. Washing, ironing, mending, taking clothes to the cleaner's or shoes to the shoemaker, can be done more efficiently in a chunk of time.
- If your schedule is regular, run laundry loads during dinner and leave your weekend *free!* Talk to your children or spouse while folding fresh clothing together.
- Clothes that don't need frequent cleaning or ironing such as wool suits are real timesavers. Think about the cleaning requirements when buying clothes for yourself and your family.
- Wrinkles in wool or silk clothes can be steamed out in the bathroom while you take a shower. But don't leave the steamy shower on too long. One unfortunate woman forgot the shower and returned to find her bathroom ceiling caved in!

- If you can't sew, or keep putting it off, find a seamstress or cleaner that will do repairs. They can sometimes help out with Halloween costumes and name tapes, too.

PERSONAL TIME

When asked how they spend their personal time, most career women/mothers will wail, "What personal time?" Indeed, it seems that each new responsibility—husband, career, child—further erodes your stock of "free" time.

Your first task is to identify free time and use it well. What about after the children go to sleep? Or early in the morning? Surely weekends hold some free time.

- Reserve one or two nights a week for household chores— ironing, sewing on name tags, mending, organizing photos, paying bills, filing insurance claims and taxes, sending out invitations. Reward yourself with truly *free* evenings on the other days.
- Organize the evening hours just as you would the day-time hours if you want to achieve the most in a short time. Set priorities!
- List things that *have* to be done and assign two or three things to each evening you're home.

Don't let your friends get lost in the shuffle of your hectic schedule. They can provide a welcome respite in busy times and a reliable support in difficult periods.

- Catch up with relatives and friends by phone after the children are in bed; especially if you have little time to get together in person. A short weekly call to close

friends, monthly or quarterly to others, can bridge the
times apart.

- Get a speaker phone or a phone with a headset if you
  spend a lot of time on the phone or if you have your
  hands occupied while talking. Opt for high quality;
  before you buy, have a friend or relative listen to you speak
  through the phone. Speakers that distort your voice or
  sound as if you're talking in a tin can or tunnel are very
  unpleasant and distracting!
- If you have friends in other cities, write a letter during
  free moments while you commute or wait in lines.
- Make lunch appointments with fellow career women.
  Plan long in advance, and don't break them. After all,
  you need to network and keep in touch.
- Remember nonworking friends. Your different lifestyles
  can provide a valuable counterpoint for each of you.
- Don't forget friends of other generations. The college
  student who needs your advice or the dear elderly lady
  down the street can be just the person to shake you out
  of your routine.

Regular exercise—daily or a few times a week—can make
a difference between lifelong fitness and flabbiness. It makes
you feel better, look better, perform better, be healthier, and
have private time to think. Here are some hints for exercis-
ing:

- Get up twenty minutes early and exercise. You can plan
  the day while you keep in shape.
- Buy an exercise video. You can fast-forward through
  some parts on an extra busy day. If you do it in the
  morning, you may find your spouse or children join-
  ing in.
- Join an aerobics class that meets several times a week
  before work, at lunch, or after work. Be sure there are

shower facilities. And check with your doctor before you make any major change in your exercise level. Most doctors will be glad to talk about this over the phone.

- Allocate time for *real* exercise on weekends. Biking, swimming, tennis, jumping rope, and many other sports can be shared with the family.
- Bicycle to and from exercise class or tennis games. It's a good warm-up and stretching exercise. Of course, commuting on bicycle is a great way to start and end the workday if it's feasible for your area.
- Swim! It's total body exercise. Don't overlook the local YWCA, which may be much less expensive than a health club.
- Jog with a portable tape player; listen to music or books on tape (available at most libraries).
- Sign up for lessons: tennis, tap dancing, gymnastics. You'll feel you're accomplishing something and getting good exercise.
- The ultimate luxury: a personal trainer at home or the office!

Some exercises can be done on the spot:

- Do neck, shoulder, and head exercises while stopped at traffic lights when you're driving.
- When you're alone at work, stand up and do a few leg and ankle exercises. This is especially easy while talking on the phone.
- If you're running late, jog to be on time!
- Use the stairs, especially up, when it's only a few flights.

Are you trying your best and still worried about not enough exercise? Consider that a career woman/parent's life is so busy and rushed that you're probably getting more exercise than you realize. Housecleaning, gardening, renovating an apartment, laundry, grocery shopping, and running after children all can be good exercise if you do them at a sprightly pace!

Personal time to relax and think is nearly as important as sleeping and eating to someone with an extremely hectic and pressured life. Schedule personal time on your calendar as you would any other appointment—and *don't break your date with yourself* even if you feel you're too busy!

> A woman in Australia reports, "For the last year I have had an arrangement with my husband whereby he takes our daughter out for dinner, or for the evening, and is responsible for putting her to bed every Wednesday night. I am not available to him for discussions or attention on Wednesday night either. The whole family knows that this is *my* night."

- Business trips—yours and your spouse's—can provide personal quiet time. Relish the solitude of business travel. Resist the temptation to fill your time with meals with colleagues and conversations with airplane seatmates. When your spouse is away, enjoy the change to set your own schedule and clear your mind.
- If you can arrange it, have your spouse take the children out for a Saturday afternoon or even a weekend from time to time. You'll be a better mother after a little time alone once in a while.

Some careers are more conducive to personal time. Says an airline stewardess, "I do all of the wonderful 'self' things on my layovers. I don't feel guilty, as I am getting paid while I'm having a layover in another city!" Teachers with long vacations, writers, artists, and others with flexible time find that they can adjust their schedules to find time for themselves.

- Learn to relax wherever you are: on the subway or bus, in the bathtub, at the table, in bed.
- Ask yourself, "Is my mouth tense? Are my shoulders tense?" and relax each muscle. Do this several times a day, and soon it will become a habit.
- Don't plan to accomplish more than is realistic. Learn to say no both in your business life and your personal life.

"Going from work to home is my inviolate quiet time. I take public transport and refuse offers of rides. During periods of stress, when I feel the need for more quiet time, I take an extra twenty minutes to have a cup of coffee in a café or browse in a shop on my way home in the evening."

Every once in a while it's worth setting aside the time (and money) to pamper yourself. Here are some suggestions:

- A manicure or pedicure.
- A massage.
- A lunch or dinner out with a friend.
- Taking the afternoon off to shop.
- A facial.
- A steam bath and sauna.
- Eating an ice cream bar.
- Buying yourself flowers.
- Or take a course in a field that really interests you. Sign up for Chinese history or physics. Go to a lecture on English gardens or puts and calls. Learning something new will focus your attention on a subject other than your troubles and you will find yourself relaxing.

While some people seem to get along on only a few hours of sleep a night, most need a solid block of sleep every night in order to function well and stay healthy—especially as they get older.

Let your body set your sleep rhythm and guard the needed hours carefully.

- Set a realistic bedtime for yourself (your spouse's may be different; so be it) and stick to it.
- If you're going to be out unusually late, have the sitter spend the night and keep the children quiet the next morning.
- Planning an early morning business trip? Say no to plans for the night before.
- Keep weekend mornings open for sleep if you see an especially busy week ahead.
- Take naps with your child. It's a lovely way to snuggle and sleep on a weekend.
- Train yourself to sleep under adverse circumstances, with noise, light, or uncomfortable space like an airline seat. You can *learn* to sleep under almost any conditions if your mind-set is positive.

If all your resolutions are for naught, you're not alone. An editor and writer says, "I know I should go to sleep earlier. I know I wouldn't feel as tired. But I enjoy the time after my kids go to sleep so much that I don't want to give up any of it. I'd rather be a little more tired the next day."

Volunteerism, an important part of the fabric of our society, is both winning and losing as a result of the flow of women into the workforce. Many women feel that they no longer have time for such "optional" activities. However, those that continue their boards and other volunteer activities often have more to offer in terms of skills and contacts.

(For complete information about the opportunities and benefits of volunteerism, see *Beyond Success: How Volunteer Service Can Help You Begin Making a Life Instead of Just a Living*, by John F. Raynolds III and Eleanor Raynolds, C.B.E. [New York: MasterMedia Limited, 1988].)

Volunteerism is one of the myriad areas where you must ask yourself if you are setting your priorities correctly. Don't be too quick to give up your community involvement. You may find that the tissue of your life, as well as the fabric of society, is the worse without it.

YOUR SPOUSE (OR IMPORTANT OTHER)

Your spouse needs to be a priority for you—and you for him—lest you find yourselves totally booked and rarely alone together.

- Have a real date regularly—if possible, once a week. It may be the only time you really have together. There is nothing like a romantic dinner to set the world right. Set aside a particular day—scheduling and remembering your "date" becomes much easier!
- When you're going out, have the sitter arrive one hour before you leave. You'll have more time to relax, get dressed, and get in a romantic mood.
- Arrange a surprise evening for two at home, with candles and soft music. Arrange for the children to be at friends' homes for dinner or overnight.
- Periodically set aside a Sunday for a surprise activity offered by one of you to the other—and be imaginative. Concerts, brunches, drives in the country, all can be delightful treats.

Impossible to squeeze in a date or an evening with your spouse? Be creative!

- Get up early and talk in bed.
- Exercise together first thing in the morning.
- Shower together.
- Make an appointment, via secretaries if necessary, for lunch once in a while or drinks between work and a business dinner.
- Once or twice a year, both of you take an afternoon off and do something you really enjoy—art galleries, movies or theater, museums, shopping, or just chatting in a café.
- Sign up for a class, club, or volunteer activity together.
- Even talking on the phone once or twice a day can help keep communication flowing in a two-career family.

"Our idea of a 'hot weekend date,'" says a public relations executive, "is to eat breakfast together and go to a noon movie." Come to think of it, that doesn't sound bad!

Weekends can be prime time with your husband. Don't let them slip away.

- Hire a regular sitter for every Saturday night if you haven't been able to establish regular weekday dates.
- Don't make the mistake of planning every Saturday with friends. Movies, concerts, theater, or dinner *alone with your husband* can be refreshing private time.
- If you don't have a sitter, plan activities at which the children can be watched without being underfoot. Have a picnic in the park; they will play at a distance while you have a quiet time eating supper together.

- Keep healthy together. Go for your annual physical together and enjoy a meal afterward. Exercise and diet *together.*
- On weekends, work as a team so that looking after things together becomes quality time.
- Weekends in the country can provide several hours of time together—the travel time in car or train. Admittedly, the little nippers are in the backseat picking up any interesting conversation, but by putting certain topics aside, a lot can be achieved in these hours.
- Daytime travel allows the passenger to read to the driver, a delightful way to share and keep up with your reading at the same time.

Vacations alone with your husband are wonderful—but many mothers feel guilty about leaving the children, and fathers feel that their one solid time with the children is vacation time.

- Why not combine the two? Go away for a romantic long weekend and have the children join you for the rest of the week. The children have something to look forward to, and you can mellow out before they arrive!
- Don't feel guilty about taking time from the children to be with your spouse. Studies show that it is the spouse, not the children, who loses time with you when you work. Try to keep a balance of private time with each.

You really have to work to keep stress at a minimum in a two-career family:

- The more tired and busy you are—the more pressure at work or outside the relationship—the more likely you are to fight. Recognize and avoid this pitfall. Avoid arguing, especially late at night if one of you is not a

night person. You may see things in an entirely different light in the morning.
- Back down; leave the room; count to ten; breathe through your nose; think before you speak.
- The sweetest words during a dispute are "I'm sorry," "You're right," "I see what you mean"—use them.
- Don't despair too soon. Several older women say that as the years roll by, arguments don't last as long and are spaced farther apart.

Says a scientist: "My favorite method (not always practical) is to go out for a fifteen-minute run when I see a fight brewing—before it has erupted. By the time I get back, I feel too good to care about whatever it was, and my husband has usually been distracted by some other activity and forgotten about it."

There is a famous cartoon in which a woman stands by the armchair of her retired husband and laments, "I married you for better or worse . . . but not for *lunch.*" Despite all the years that you both suffered from the lack of free time, coping with an unemployed or retired spouse is not easy, especially if you are still working. The role reversal can set up an uncomfortable feeling for one or both of you. Each may be jealous of the other. (For advice on how to cope with employment changes of all sorts, see *Out the Organization: Gaining the Competitive Edge,* by Madeleine and Robert Swain [New York: MasterMedia Limited, 1988].)

If your spouse has been fired:

- Suggest temporary work until the "ideal" job can be found.

- Never blame. Positive thinking will help in his job search.
- Deal with your own anger or disappointment. Then you'll be able to support him wholeheartedly.
- Help your husband in his job search. You can help keep logs of people called, type letters, be a cheerleader.
- Use your own network. You never know who might have a lead.

If your spouse has retired:

- Some men have a strong desire to be the breadwinner. Stress the continuing contribution that he's making to the family in terms of child-rearing (these may be grandchildren), household management, and your peace of mind.
- Suggest that he take up old or new hobbies—things he would have loved to do had he had time in the past.
- One of his hobbies might well turn into a postretirement career. If something looks promising, urge your spouse to try to turn a skill into a business, especially if he misses his working days.
- If money is tight, keep working. It's very reassuring to have a dependable income if it looks as if retirement benefits and Social Security might not be quite enough. In this situation, a second career for your husband becomes more attractive.

RELIEVING STRESS

We know all about stress—hectic schedules, complicated responsibilities at home, never enough time, pressures of all kinds to perform well on the job. Elsewhere in this book, we have talked about the necessity of establishing priorities in your life—of the importance of *not* trying to succeed at everything every day.

You can't do everything all at once—some aspects of your life will have to wait their turn to become the focus of your attention. You may be on a fast track at the office, with teenaged children, or maybe you're juggling a part-time job and have to deal with two kids under five. Whatever your situation, you probably don't have enough time to accomplish everything you want to do. Hence, stress at home and at the office.

- Learn to recognize what causes you stress. Everyone is not affected in the same way by an event or personality. You may not be bothered in the least by a boss who shouts and who has a hair-trigger temper. On the other hand, sulking may drive you crazy. You may thrive on deadlines but be unable to deal with an amorphous project. Identify the stressors that really bother you. Try writing down a list over the next week, as they come up.
- Learn to separate the garden-variety anxieties that arise in most common work situations from truly difficult problems. If you are so stressed or depressed that you don't think you can overcome a difficulty by yourself, go to an expert: for office problems, the appropriate person may be in your corporation—someone in the human resources department or your supervisor. For personal problems, turn to a physician or therapist.
- Recognize the source of stress and deal with it; then develop techniques that enable you to relax. Learn to control your emotions and attitudes—your outlook—so that sources of stress cease to affect you in a damaging way. Think positively.
- Try to get in touch with your feelings. Why do you dislike your supervisor so much? He's not such a bad

fellow, and seems to like you and your work perfectly well. Other people seem to like him. Does he remind you of your Uncle Harry, whom you loathe? Does his office smell like cigars?

- You might be stuck in a truly awful work situation. Do you have an impossible boss? Are you expected to do the work of two employees because of cutbacks? Have you inherited a difficult assistant whom you just *don't like* but whom you have no real reason to fire? A close friend or spouse may be able to help by letting you talk out the problem as you try to find ways to cope.
- Try to solve problems yourself by talking frankly with the co-workers who are making your life a misery. Sometimes you can improve a situation by clearing up a misunderstanding. Sometimes there is more bluster than reality, and a bully, when faced down, will often retreat.
- You might talk with management if you can't solve your problems yourself. You risk irritating some higher-ups, of course, who might think that the person you're complaining about is just great. But sometimes a supervisor can help—by giving you a new assistant, or interceding with your boss, or helping to rearrange your work responsibilities.
- It is a positive step to try to improve your lot, but sometimes a stressful situation just can't be fixed. Accept that hard fact, work on dealing with the stress you can't eliminate, and start looking for a new job.
- You may be working too hard, and not giving your mind a moment to rest or your body a chance to unwind. Sitting in a tight coil day after day in your office, worrying and working, is going to backfire. Anxiety will feed on itself. You have to learn to break the pattern.
- Change is a great stress reliever. Change your focus, and your problems may seem less important.
- For small stresses, get out of the office, go for a walk,

telephone a friend. For more major tension, go to the zoo, get a haircut, meet your spouse for lunch.

- Make sure that you eat something that will give you energy and nutrition. A hungry person is a sensitive person; if you feel headachy and cranky, sometimes something simple but restorative, like a glass of milk or a piece of fruit, will work wonders.
- Get extra sleep until the situation at work clears up. You must be rested if you're going to resist the pressure of the day. Recognize that stress will leave you more tired than usual, and rethink your bedtime.
- Exercise in the office or outside. It makes you think about something other than your problems. It also gets your pulse rate up and more oxygen into your blood. Strenuous exercise has a tranquilizing effect on most people.
- Learn to relax in the office. There are all sorts of mind-clearing techniques, biofeedback, meditation, or prayer. If you can learn to induce relaxation at will, a stressful situation at work can be defused as soon as it happens.

Balance in life is not just a good idea, it's a necessity. You may be able to work eighteen-hour days when you're twenty-five, but what about when you're thirty-five, or forty-five? Magazines and TV talk shows often describe burnout—fast-track executives who drop out under the strain of trying to stay on top at the office, and yet have a satisfying personal life as well.

You may not be able to do it all—not everything at once, anyway. Balance means changing and sequencing your priorities as necessary. These might be the years that you have a less-than-demanding career—perhaps to be replaced by all-out ladder-climbing when your children are twelve and fourteen.

No matter what your career and personal goals, be flexible enough to step back from your work. Your health will be better, and so will your mental outlook—not to mention the beneficial effects on your spouse and children.

Time away from the office—whether for your six-year-old's debut as a mushroom in the class play or a getaway vacation in Bermuda with your spouse—is necessary to keep balance in your life and equilibrium in your family.

Many women *never* ask for time off; many never take a vacation; and a significant percentage only take time off when they are practically forced to by higher management. The life of a workaholic is not a sensible choice even if the fast track is very important to you. If you want a husband and family, you must take the time to build and maintain those relationships.

The best approach to taking time off is to plan well ahead, covering all bases with contingency plans that ought to take care of any problem that might arise while you're gone. A few things to keep in mind:

- Don't feel guilty. You *need* time away from work to recharge, whether it's for two weeks, a long weekend, or an afternoon.
- Obviously, if you're well organized, it will be easier to get away. Keep up to date, maintain your files and schedules in excellent shape—so that a colleague can deal with a problem when you're out of the office.
- For longer vacations, plan as if you're a seasoned general going into battle. Don't leave unfinished business: all reports must be done, all projects in the works, all work assigned.
- If you work for the sort of person who is nervous when managers are away, be sure that you also spell out your staff arrangements for keeping projects moving along smoothly. Prepare a written schedule if necessary.

- This is the time to make good use of that reliable, talented staff you've put in place. Give careful instructions, making sure that each person understands his or her duties and responsibilities. Set deadlines.
- Leave someone in charge. This is no time for democracy; it could turn into anarchy.
- Leave your itinerary and phone numbers. You may never get a call, but emergencies do arise. If you need to keep in close touch, try to call in at the same time every day or every other day. Your staff will then be ready with their questions and reports.
- When all your plans have been made, put them in writing. Send copies to everyone who will be concerned with scheduling while you're away—especially your boss.
- Have your staff mail you any important reports or memos that you need to read before your return. You can go through them at the airport or on the plane.
- When you return from your trip, you should be able to pick up the work of that day and not have to be preoccupied with everything that came up during the past two weeks.

It's up to you to make time for yourself and to be with those who are important to you. The more balance and less stress in your life, the more effective you will be and the better you will be able to manage it all.

CHAPTER TEN

Alternatives

Companies are gradually coming around to the realization that women are an important factor in the workforce and that the right benefits packages and flexibility can attract and retain the best women employees.

BENEFITS PACKAGES

Benefits packages are a key compensation factor in many jobs. The traditional benefits such as insurance, sick days, and vacations are being supplemented by in-house day care, optional extra time off, and other benefits suited to the working parent.

- If your husband is covered for certain benefits at his work, be sure that your coverage dovetails. For example, one of you might drop a duplicate health insurance benefit.
- In some cases, it's worth having both of you carry family medical and dental coverage. For example, one com-

216

pany may cover regular dental checkups while the other pays higher amounts for each procedure. If you anticipate expenses such as psychiatric counseling to exceed the maximum at one insurance company, the other may pick up the balance.

- A "cafeteria benefits package" is ideal for a working parent. It allows the employee to select among a "menu" of benefits. The company offers a stated dollar value of benefits. You customize your own package, concentrating on those benefits that you especially need. You sometimes can choose additional sick days or more vacation time, which can be spent with your family as part of a cafeteria benefits package.

- Some employers allow you to use *your* sick leave to stay home if a child or elderly dependent is ill. This can be a very important benefit if you have many children or a chronically ill child or adult to care for. If you're not sure if this benefit is available, ask!

- Under "cumulative service" programs, companies base seniority on cumulative service rather than consecutive employment. Thus, you might take time off—even a few years—to be with your children or tend to other pressing family matters and yet not lose your chance at promotion or your accruing of years toward your pension. Companies that provide this benefit make every effort to find a suitable position for the returning employee, at the same level as the previous job.

MATERNITY LEAVE

The minimum standard paid maternity leave is "two weeks before the due date and six weeks after the birth of the baby." Thus, if your baby is born on the due date, you will have eight uninterrupted paid weeks of leave. If your baby is born *before* your due date, you forfeit some or all of the prebirth leave. If the baby is late, you have a pay gap from the due date until the birth. Generally, there is a job guarantee for at least two or three months so that you can return to your job after your leave.

Many companies are offering more generous paid maternity leaves and also paternity leaves at the time of the birth of the child. You should be knowledgeable about your company's policies:

- In a large company, maternity leave policies should be clearly documented and readily available. The personnel office should be able to provide this information.
- In smaller companies where maternity leave policies are not cast in stone, you can be instrumental in designing a fair and generous policy. You will be doing yourself and your employer a favor.
- If a medical condition requires you to take off more time than your employer is willing to pay for, you may be eligible for disability pay from your state. The amounts are not large, but you have earned the right to these benefits and should take advantage.
- If your company is reluctant to hold your job for a period of months during your leave, it may be up to you to offer a viable solution: allocating your job among fellow employees, suggesting temps or consultants, making yourself available by phone or in person for a few hours a week. Be creative if you want to return to your job—but don't give up your maternity leave.
- In some fields, holding a position open for several months is truly difficult: an actress starring in a play, a chief executive officer, a first grade teacher. Here the key is planning: timing your pregnancy and/or your career responsibilities to allow success in both.

- If you are interviewing for jobs and you fear that questioning the details of the maternity leave policy may jeopardize your chances, wait until after you've been given a job offer. But don't hesitate to ask when deciding whether or not to accept the job. They won't withdraw the offer!

MAKING YOUR JOB FIT YOUR NEEDS

We've talked about having it all, but maybe not all at once. Perhaps a nine-to-five job is not right for you at the moment. If your children need more of you, if you're responsible for the care of an ill or elderly parent, finishing a screenplay, trying to get a new business off the ground, restoring a Victorian house—you might want to search for the sort of job that permits an alternative time commitment.

"I am very happy with my husband and children and consequently have had the incentive to limit my career ambitions to what I can reasonably achieve at this time in my life while giving priority to my family's needs. I concluded that there could not be two time-consuming careers in our family while the children were young and made a conscious decision to control my working hours and bear the career consequences of such a decision.

"Because of the nature of my work and my position as a partner in a small law firm, I have flexibility in my day. I can usually structure my day so that I can attend school events. I can occasionally go uptown to pick up a child at preschool for lunch or my elementary school child for an afternoon outing."

If you find a less-than-full-time job, you may be effectively removing yourself from the *fastest* track, at least for the moment; but you're keeping your hand in and staying current. That will make it much easier when you decide that it's time to concentrate a larger percentage of your energy on your career once again.

You should know when to slow down. If the demands of your job, children, home, and other responsibilities are too much for you, stress, poor performance at work, and frazzled temper at home may be the result. Rather than burning out and having all aspects of your life suffer, take the steps necessary to make your job fit your needs. The change need not be permanent; a few months or years of an alternative schedule may suffice.

There is a wide range of alternatives to full-time work. Consider them all in light of the nature of your work and the other demands on your time.

Part-time Work

There are variations on part-time work that you should consider.

- As a *permanent* part-time worker, you do not work a full week, but your days or hours are predetermined and you usually give your employer the equivalent of three or four full days. You are normally entitled to benefits, and can switch back to full-time with relative ease.
- You may elect to take a part-time occasional job as your schedule permits you to take an assignment. A lawyer might be hired on a case-by-case basis, or a doctor or nurse might fill in for vacationing permanent staff. While this type of part-time work affords maximum flexibility, you give up the assurance of a regular pay-

check and the benefits available to a permanent employee.

Workers in many fields have managed to take advantage of part-time schedules: secretaries, educators, researchers, artists, editors, librarians, accountants, and bankers. With corporations cutting back all across the country, part-time work can be beneficial to the employer as well. By making a previously full-time job part-time, the company can hire a *more*-qualified person for the same cost or the same-level person for *lower* cost.

- If your position is based on a fund of experience or knowledge rather than your physical presence at all times, you may be able to switch to part-time and keep your current job.
- If your job is not suited to part-time, be creative and find a slot in your firm that *can* be part-time. Few companies have positions specifically designated as part-time. Traditionally, most part-time jobs in large companies have been staff functions rather than jobs with responsibility for bottom-line profit, although even this distinction is changing rapidly.
- When considering part-time work, be sure that the job really *can* be done in the time allocated. Many women find themselves with part-time salaries and full-time jobs, as they work late, take home work, and go to work on days off!
- If you cut back to three days a week, don't automatically assume that you should only receive 60 percent of your salary. If you are really doing most of the work of a full-timer but more efficiently, you may be able to do better than a straight percentage cut.
- Force yourself to stick to your schedule, be it Monday/Wednesday/Friday or daily until 2:00 P.M. Your clients,

co-workers, and boss need to *know* when they can count
on you. If your daughter's school play falls on a workday,
you may find yourself *less* able to take off an afternoon
than a full-time employee.
- Similarly, stick to your guns about really not working on
your days off. You chose part-time because you needed
the time for other activities or responsibilities. Don't
waste this sought-after opportunity.

The Big Eight accounting firm Touche Ross is experimenting with a four-day workweek for mothers of
young children who want to stay on the partnership
track. The short-week path takes ten to twelve years
rather than the traditional eight to ten years, but keeps
women in the running for top management.

Job-sharing

- Job-sharing is another variation on part-time work. You
would work only part-time, and someone else would
cover the same job during the time that you're not in the
office.
- If *being available* is important in your job—for example,
a salesperson or receptionist—each person can work
half time, with one starting when the other ends.
- If your job requires follow-up and sharing of ideas, close
cooperation of the job-sharers is necessary. Typically,
each person would work three days, with one day of
overlap (one hour of overlap if each *day* is shared). This
type of sharing is suited to managers of people or products, teachers, librarians, and clergy.

- Whether there is an overlap or not, be sure you get along well with your partner. Your work will reflect on each other, and you will surely be required to patch up each other's blunders or rush to catch up each other's projects from time to time. Mutual respect and cooperation are key.

Flextime

This option allows employees to work full-time but to choose alternative hours of arrival and departure. In some companies, there are "core" hours when all staff are meant to be on the job, but you have leeway, perhaps two hours at the beginning and the end of the day. For example, you could work 7:00 to 3:00, or 11:00 to 7:00, instead of the traditional 9:00 to 5:00.

- If you want to be at home when your children get home from school, flextime can be ideal. Even tiny children can get themselves ready in the morning with a little help from Dad if you've taken the 6:03 A.M. to work. And you'll be home by 3:30 to be a Girl Scout leader.
- Late hours suit some schedules. If you are an avid horseback rider, free time in the morning may be important. Parents of teenagers often find that the children aren't home until late anyway, so they may attempt to adjust to the late-to-bed/late-to-rise schedule of their teenage children.
- Another version of flextime allows an employee to work shorter hours one day and make up the time the next. Perhaps the idea of working a ten-hour day for four days a week appeals to you. Many companies are having great success with this type of tailor-made schedule for employees.

Temporary Work

To maximize flexibility, temporary work can provide the best solution. Office temporaries, substitute teachers, seasonal help in stores, all enjoy the ability to decide when and how much to work.

- If you have good office skills—you know word processing, for example—temporary office work may be a suitable choice. You can work full- or half-days at your option, and avoid the stress of a permanent job.
- If you can find your own office temporary assignments, you don't forfeit the large percentage claimed by office temporary agencies. For example, former employers might call you in to substitute for employees who are ill or on vacation, due to your knowledge of the company.
- If you are unsure what field might interest you as a career in the future—advertising versus banking, for example—temporary work can provide a bird's-eye view on various industries. If you let your temporary boss know of your interest in pursuing the field, you may even have a source of a summer job or internship in the future.
- Temporary teachers often find themselves so much in demand that the desired time off is more a dream than a reality. You should decide in advance how much you wish to work and stick to your decision.

Working at Home

Working at home has been a traditional benefit for writers, jewelry designers, tutors, and piano teachers. Now, with the advent of the computer terminal, whole new categories of work are opening up. Computer programmers, bankers, analysts, researchers, and students all can work at home.

- Successfully working at home requires a space conducive to work and uninterrupted time to concentrate. Even if you don't have a spare room for an office or studio, pick a spot in your home where you will work and declare it "off bounds," at least while you're working.
- If you have been using a computer terminal at your office, explore the possibility of having your company install a system in your home. You can be a full-time employee of your corporation or institution, with full pay and benefits, if you work a full schedule and report in on a regular basis.

Consulting and Free-lancing

If you have an acknowledged area of expertise, try consulting or free-lancing. Former employers, clients, or others in your field can provide consulting contracts to suit your schedule and financial needs. Since you provide expertise without the cost to your employer of office, benefits, and other overhead, you can expect to be quite well paid—at or above the level of an equivalent employee in many industries. Of course, you are responsible for "selling" yourself and for buying your own benefits packages. It's a high-risk/high-reward solution.

Your Own Business

If you start your own business, whether a mail-order firm, design studio, or dog-grooming salon, you are the boss and you can keep whatever flexible hours you want. You can even take the baby to work.

- Be advised that most entrepreneurs put in *much longer* hours than they ever did while working for a company. Be sure you're prepared for a great deal of work before launching a small business.
- Starting a small business also entails a financial commitment that may strain your family's budget if you are not strict about setting limits and keeping costs down. Be realistic before you start investing your time and money in a new venture. Also, be prepared to call it quits before you are overextended if it turns out not to be a viable business. Know how to cut your losses.
- If you are running your new business from your home, create a professional atmosphere conducive to business. Screaming children in the background will not impress potential clients. Get or make (on the word processor) stationery and business cards. A separate business line on the phone is important. As soon as you can afford a copying machine and computer, take advantage of these timesaving tools.

DROPPING OUT

Are you finding that managing it all just isn't working for you? Many women find that they can't, or don't want to, manage it all at certain points in their life. A decision to take a break need not be the end of your career! Here are some thoughts on dropping out, at least temporarily.

Most mothers relish the weeks or months of maternity leave as a special time to bond with the baby. Make the most of it:

- Realize that you will be tired and very occupied with the baby. Don't make unrealistic plans for yourself and your family.

- Establish the time frame of your leave at the outset so that when you return to work, you'll have plenty of time for the adjustment.
- Have competent child care begin at least a week before you begin work so that you are sure that the transition back to work will go smoothly. It's usually the mother, not the baby, that suffers most from the return to work!
- If you don't feel comfortable with the six weeks or two months that your company offers, let them know right away that you want an extended parental leave. It's fairer and easier to discuss this before the baby is born than to wait until a few days before you're due back to work.

You may feel like extending your maternity leave or just taking off time for your family or other activities. Some companies permit such "personal" leaves of absence. Establish in your own mind the following before you ask for a leave:

- *How long a leave do you want?* If you're not sure, ask for the maximum time permitted. Better to return early than to need an extension once you're gone.
- *When do you want to start?* Don't respond "Immediately" unless there's an imminent crisis. Why not start in a few months, when there's been time for transition?
- *How will the transition take place?* In most cases, your job will be given to someone else. Who? How will they be trained?
- *How will you notify your staff and colleagues?* You can cite personal reasons without giving unduly detailed explanations. Most people respect the fact that you have set your priorities and are acting accordingly.
- Evaluate the strength of your position at work and your need or desire for a leave. Don't ask for a leave unless you are prepared to quit if they don't agree to it. They may just offer you the "alternative" of resigning.

- If you are well respected and valuable at work, and if you are granted a leave, live up to your reputation by keeping informed and in touch during your leave.

If a family or medical emergency necessitates the leave, some of these niceties may slide—but try to tie up the loose ends after the worst of the emergency has passed.

> "Since I took my leave of absence, my children have all blossomed and life is much less chaotic for my husband and me as well. But I do miss the stimulation and sense of power which I had in my career. At work, if you say, 'Please redo this five-year plan before Friday morning,' *it will be done.* At home, if you say 'Please pick up this sneaker before dinner,' *it won't!*"

If you are taking time off, be it maternity leave, personal leave, or resigning, *enjoy it.* Above all, don't feel guilty. Your decision was surely made in light of the many facets of your life that must be juggled. If your reasons are sound and you take advantage of the time off, you will one day be better prepared to return to your career or to start another.

Knowing yourself, setting your goals and priorities, following through with careful planning, balancing your family and work, making time for friends and yourself, controlling stress, knowing when and if you need to slow down—these are the elements that will make you successful at *managing it all.*

APPENDIX I

What Is Your Time Management Style?

Are you the *analyst,* the *juggler,* or the *philosopher?* Answer twenty-five questions about how you manage your time. Then score yourself to find your dominant and secondary time management style. Circle the letter corresponding to your answer.

1. A. You have breakfast on the run; read or work during breakfast.
   B. You have breakfast at home with the family.
2. A. You select clothes the night before based on the weather forecast and your schedule.
   B. You select clothes in the morning based on your mood and the weather.
3. A. You almost always have lunch plans, business or personal.
   B. You prefer business-related lunches, with clients or colleagues.
   C. You like a break at lunch, alone or with friends.
4. A. You dislike interruptions like phone calls or drop-in visits.
   B. You refuse interruptions. Ask them to call back or come back.
   C. You don't mind interruptions, but often keep people waiting or "on hold."

5. A. Your desk is neat, with only current projects visible.
   B. Your desk is covered with projects in various stages of completion.
6. A. You arrive at work and leave work on time.
   B. You arrive and leave late.
   C. You arrive and leave at various hours based on commitments.
7. A. You often stay up late working on an interesting project.
   B. You go to bed at a regular hour.
8. A. When there's pressure at work, family and friends have to take a backseat.
   B. You always have time for family and friends.
9. When you're on the phone, you:
   A. Doodle, read memos, neaten your desk drawer.
   B. Listen attentively; imagine the caller in his or her setting.
   C. Keep the call brief; take notes; concentrate.
10. When you're busy and you're asked to take on a new responsibility:
    A. You can't say NO.
    B. You don't say NO; you say LATER.
    C. You say NO.
11. A. You can concentrate very well and rarely get distracted.
    B. You are often distracted, but can get back to work easily.
    C. You have difficulty getting back to work when distracted.
12. A. You like clear-cut projects and near-term deadlines.
    B. You like generalized guidelines and long-term deadlines.
    C. You dislike guidelines and deadlines.
13. A. You take work home and do personal items at work.
    B. You keep a separation—work at work; personal items at home.
14. As a supervisor, you:
    A. Check up on employees regularly: daily or weekly.
    B. Check up on employees frequently throughout the day.
    C. Wait for employees to come to you.
15. People are impressed by how:
    A. Thoughtful and considerate you are.
    B. Reliable you are.
    C. Energetic you are.

16. A. You dislike pressure.
    B. You ignore pressure.
    C. You thrive on pressure.
17. A. You set up back-to-back meetings.
    B. You leave time between meetings in case you're running late.
    C. You schedule only one meeting in the morning and one in the afternoon.
18. A. Your files and drawers are neat; others can access materials easily.
    B. Your files and drawers are in á state that only you understand.
19. If you have no lunch plans, you:
    A. Eat alone and work.
    B. Eat alone and relax.
    C. Quickly arrange something.
20. A. You keep long lists of things to do this week.
    B. You keep short, prioritized lists of things to do today.
    C. You avoid written lists; keep priorities in mind.
21. People like having you on their team because:
    A. You are diligent and well organized.
    B. You are pleasant to be with and a calming influence.
    C. You work fast and take on a lot of responsibility.
22. Your solutions to problems tend to be:
    A. Thoughtful and studied.
    B. Tightly analyzed and well demonstrated.
    C. Speedy and original.
23. Your vacations are:
    A. Packed with adventure.
    B. Very relaxing; a total break.
    C. Original and interesting.
24. Your pocketbook and briefcase are:
    A. Stuffed with papers and other items.
    B. Very neat.
25. Your children and/or spouse complain because:
    A. You're never there; too busy with other things.
    B. You get mad if they interrupt you.
    C. You talk too much.

SCORE YOURSELF

Transfer your responses to the score sheet by circling the letters next to each question number. If a letter appears twice, circle both.

	Analyst	*Juggler*	*Philosopher*
1.	B	A	B
2.	A	B	B
3.	B	A	C
4.	A	C	B
5.	A	B	A or B
6.	A	B	C
7.	B	A	A
8.	A	A	B
9.	C	A	B
10.	C	A	B
11.	C	B	A
12.	A	B	C
13.	B	A	B
14.	A	B	C
15.	B	C	A
16.	A	C	B
17.	B	A	C
18.	A	B	A
19.	A	C	B
20.	B	A	C
21.	A	C	B
22.	B	C	A
23.	B	A	C
24.	B	A	A or B
25.	B	A	C

TOTAL   _____   _____   _____

SCORING

Over 20   You are too extreme in this category. Look for opportunities to develop the other two styles.

15–20   This is your dominant style. Make the most of the positive aspects of this style and avoid the pitfalls.

10–14   You don't have a dominant style. Draw yje best from your two major styles and recognize possible conflicts between the two.

5–9   These are your subordinate styles. Use them when they serve you well.

Under 5   These styles are underdeveloped. Work on using them appropriately.

If you are an *analyst*, then you:

Work on one task at a time.
Finish one job completely before beginning another.
Compile lists of tasks; make detailed plans.
Maintain neat files and records.
Fit well in a large organization.
Are considered easy to work with, a good team member.
Dislike interruptions.
Have a hard time getting moving.
Can get paralyzed under stress.

As a *juggler,* you:

Like to have many balls in the air at once.
Have high energy and high output.
Have developed a successful professional style.
May have trouble delegating.
Suffer from "lost" items—missing papers, forgotten appointments.
Are frustrating to work with.

And if you score high in the *philosopher* category, then you:

    Appear to have plenty of time for all tasks.
    Give full attention to people.
    Are a calming influence.
    Are thoughtful, and figure out solutions carefully.
    Have a style conducive to successful relationships.
    Risk appearing to have low energy and low output.
    Are not viewed as an achiever.

APPENDIX II

You and Child Care

Good child care is a working mother's greatest concern. Your choice will depend on your:

- Geographical location
- Kind of help available
- Income
- Philosophy of child-rearing
- The company you work for
- Ingenuity

WHERE TO FIND QUALIFIED HELP

1. Nurse registries
2. Baby-sitting agencies
3. By asking your obstetrician, pediatrician, neighbors, friends, church or temple
4. State licensing agencies
5. Newspaper advertisements
6. Local college or university personnel department employment agencies

7. Foreign student exchange
8. Local theater or dance troupe
9. Retiree center
10. Yellow Pages under "child care"

CHILD-CARE OPTIONS

Public-Supported Day Care

Advantage:	Subsidized.
	Teachers, food, playroom.
Disadvantage:	Limited number of facilities.
	Few accept infants.
	Don't spend much on food, facilities, or staff.
	Strict schedules (not flexible).
	Quality of day care can vary.

Employer-Supported Day Care

Advantage:	Company usually pays half the cost of maintaining the facility, so cost to the parents can be as low as $25 a week.
	Some corporate day care centers are also open to children from the community at the same low fee.
	Parents can visit during the day.
	Teachers, food, playroom.
Disadvantage:	Limited number of facilities.
	Few accept infants.
	Strict schedules/not flexible.

Church-Affiliated Day Care/Private Company Day Care

Advantage: Teachers, food, playroom.
Disadvantage: Considerably more expensive (fee for infant care
                can run as high as $140/week).
                Few accept infants.
                Strict schedules/not flexible.
                May not be a convenient location.

Child Care at Baby-Sitter's Home
(Relative, Friend, Professional)

Advantage: Less expensive than church/private day care cen-
                ters.
                Usually have playroom and food.
                More flexible.
                Homelike setting.
                Located in residential neighborhood; therefore,
                often easier to get to.
Disadvantage: Many are not licensed or regulated, so health and
                safety standards can be lax.
                Quality of day care can vary.

In-House Child Care (Housekeeper, Nanny, Relative,
Student in Exchange for Room and Board,
Grandmother, Grandfather, Father, Retiree)

Advantage: Individual attention for child.
                Less stressful for child than taking to day care
                center.
                Can be well-trained, competent professional.
                Can provide you the most support and the least
                worry.

Disadvantage: May not be well-trained, competent professional (trained professionals are expensive—the salaries of nannies can run as high as $15,000 a year; not all of them live in, but if yours does, you'll be paying room and board as well).

Family relationships can be fragile, so you may find it is better to deal with a stranger who can be corrected or fired with a minimum of unpleasant consequences than using a relative.

QUESTIONS TO CONSIDER WHEN CHOOSING DAY CARE

1. Can you get to the center easily from your office or home?
2. What are your hours? Are they rigid or flexible? If you are detained, will a staff member remain with your child or will you have to arrange for someone to pick him or her up at the specified hour?
3. Is the establishment licensed? If applicable, are the personnel certified? If they are not, what are their qualifications?
4. What will be done in the event of an emergency? Is there a qualified doctor or nurse available on short notice? What about a nearby hospital?
5. What has been the health record for both staff and children?
6. What meals are provided? Who prepares them and where does the food come from?
7. What is the facility's vacation schedule? Will it be closed on holidays or during the summer?
8. How many children are cared for and what is the ratio of staff to children? Is it constant or is it likely to change?
9. What is the policy on naps? Are mats provided for that purpose?

QUESTIONS TO CONSIDER WHEN CHOOSING A CAREGIVER

1. Why are they working as housekeepers/nurses/nannies/baby-sitters? Is it a career or an interim position?
2. What is their basic child care philosophy? Are they rigid in this philosophy? Be specific—for example, ask specific "what if" questions about how to handle situations. "What would you do if the baby fell out of the high chair but appeared to be all right?"
3. How might they take direction/correction from the parent?
4. How would they handle their own possible disapproval of the parents' actions? For example, if the working mother is delayed at the office, and the child is old enough to understand, would the caregiver be supportive of the mother's dilemma and reassure the child about the mother's imminent return?
5. What does the caregiver consider his/her strengths or weaknesses to be?
6. Is the caregiver healthy? Any back trouble? Will he/she be able to manage lifting growing children?
7. What is the caregiver's educational background? Any nurse's training?
8. What do they consider the proper requirements of the job? Does it include doing the baby's laundry? The family laundry? Cleaning the baby's room? Cooking for the baby? For the family?
9. What salary and benefits are they expecting? Will they want to be paid by cash or check?
10. How flexible are they about time off, and what vacation time would they expect? Do they want pay if you take a vacation?
11. Do they drive? Have they ever had an accident? Have they ever driven with infants or small children in the car?
12. Are they familiar with the area in which you live?

CHECKING REFERENCES

Be sure to ask a prospective caregiver for references and check each one. Try to talk to previous employers at some length. This is the only way to be certain you are hiring someone reliable. If you are not wholly satisfied—even if you cannot put your finger on why—pass up the applicant.

Here are questions to ask:

1. What were the applicant's strengths? Weaknesses? General capabilities?
2. Was he/she reliable? Argumentative? Intrusive in the day-to-day workings of the family?
3. Was the applicant flexible with time arrangements?
4. Was the applicant comfortable with the child/children? How did the child respond?
5. Did the applicant take directions? Did he/she follow the parents' wishes?
6. Did the previous employers feel secure leaving their children with the applicant?
7. Was the applicant discreet?
8. Was the applicant ever ill or did she have personal problems that prevented the fulfillment of regular duties?
9. If English is not the applicant's native tongue, is her comprehension adequate?
10. Were there any special problems? (Try to get the previous employers to be straightforward. Point out that this person will be the sole caregiver for your child for a large part of each day.)
11. How did the applicant handle emergencies?
12. Why did the applicant leave their employ?

ABOUT THE AUTHORS

Beverly Benz Treuille, a vice president of Citibank, has been a pioneer among women in management. She has successfully combined career (as a part-time vice president for many years) and motherhood (with three young children). A Harvard M.B.A., corporate board member, and president of a nonprofit agency, she is a dynamic example that *Managing It All* is possible.

Susan Schiffer Stautberg, the author of *Pregnancy Nine to Five* and *The Pregnancy and Motherhood Diary: Planning the First Year of Your Second Career,* has written articles and op-ed pieces for numerous national business publications and women's magazines. Now an entrepreneur in publishing, she has been a Washington TV bureau chief, a White House fellow, as well as a communications executive with a Fortune 500 company and a Big Eight accounting firm.

Additional copies of *Managing It All* may be ordered by sending a check for $9.95 (including postage and handling) to:

MasterMedia Limited
333 West 52nd Street
Suite 306
New York, NY 10019
(212) 246–9500

The authors are available for keynotes, half-day and full-day seminars and workshops. Please contact MasterMedia for availability and fee arrangements.

OTHER MASTERMEDIA BOOKS

The Pregnancy and Motherhood Diary: Planning the First Year of Your Second Career, by Susan Schiffer Stautberg, is the first and only undated appointment diary that shows how to manage pregnancy and career. ($12.95 spiralbound)

Cities of Opportunity: Finding the Best Place to Work, Live and Prosper in the 1990's and Beyond, by Dr. John Tepper Marlin, explores the job and living options for the next decade and into the next century. This consumer guide and handbook, written by one of the world's experts on cities, selects and features forty-six American cities and metropolitan areas. ($13.95 paper and $24.95 cloth)

The Dollars and Sense of Divorce, by Dr. Judith Briles, is the first book to combine practical tips on overcoming the legal hurdles and planning finances before, during, and after divorce. ($10.95 paper)

Out the Organization: Gaining the Competitive Edge, by Madeleine and Robert Swain, is written for the millions of Americans whose jobs are no longer safe, whose companies are not loyal, and who face futures of uncertainty. It gives advice on finding a new job or starting your own business. ($17.95 cloth)

Aging Parents and You: A Complete Handbook to Help You Help Your Elders Maintain a Healthy, Productive and Independent Life, by Eugenia Anderson-Ellis and Marsha Dryan, is a complete guide to providing care to aging relatives. It gives practical advice and resources to the adults who are helping their elders lead productive and independent lives. ($9.95 paper)

Beyond Success: How Volunteer Service Can Help You Begin Making a Life Instead of Just a Living, by John F. Raynolds III and Eleanor Raynolds, C.B.E., is a unique how-to book targeted to business and professional people considering volunteer work, senior citizens who wish to fill leisure time meaningfully, and students trying out various career options. The book is filled with interviews with celebrities, CEOs, and average citizens who talk about the benefits of service work. ($19.95 cloth)

Criticism in Your Life: How to Give It, How to Take It, How to Make It Work for You, by Dr. Deborah Bright, offers practical advice, in an upbeat, readable, and realistic fashion, for turning criticism into control. Charts and diagrams guide the reader into managing criticism from bosses, spouses, relationships, children, friends, neighbors, and in-laws. ($17.95 cloth)